SOLZHENITSYN'S RELIGION

SOLZHENITSYN'S RELIGION

Niels C. Nielsen, Jr.

THOMAS NELSON INC., Publishers

NASHVILLE
NEW YORK

Published by Thomas Nelson, Inc., Nashville, Tennessee
Manufactured in the United States of America

Library of Congress Cataloging in Publication Data

Nielsen, Niels Christian, 1921–
  Solzhenitsyn's religion.

  Includes bibliographical references.
  1. Solzhenitsyn, Aleksandr Isaevich, 1918–
Religion and ethics.   I. Title.
PG3488.04Z79   891.7'8'4409   75–11980
ISBN 0–8407–5091–9
ISBN 0–8407–5598–8 pbk.

Contents

Preface

What words can be used to describe Professor Nielsen's book on Alexander Solzhenitsyn's religion? Words such as *exciting, relevant, illuminating,* and *helpful* come to mind.

The American public, this writer included, has had wide exposure to Solzhenitsyn. *The Gulag Archipelago* is a best-seller. But we do not have perspective—especially in relation to his religion. In more general terms, we need more understanding of the milieu in which Solzhenitsyn lived and wrote in the USSR.

Professor Nielsen has the intellectual and practical travel and study background for providing us with the book we need. He also has the gift of communicating profound material in a clear-cut and readable style. For many of us, his *The Layman Looks at World Religions* is a classic in terms of communication.

The writer of this Preface has made two trips to the USSR and anticipates taking two study groups in the summer of 1975. This book should furnish excellent background reading for all those who have been or hope to go to Russia. For illumination of the life and writings of Solzhenitsyn, a fascinating portrayal is given of much of the recent religious, literary, philosophical, and political history of Russia.

It should be helpful to list some of the specific features of the book which constitute its strength and appeal.

1. The material is interesting and dramatic. The style is popular and informal. Universal themes are considered in

terms of concrete and specific examples. An amazing amount of factual material about Russia is contained in the book. Anecdotes enliven the material. In other words, it is both informative and interesting. It shows a wide critical acquaintance with authors who have written in the field of recent Russian religious and cultural life.

2. The relation of Solzhenitsyn to Dostoevsky, Tolstoy, Pasternak, Sakharov, and other prominent Russian thinkers and literary figures is helpful. Chapter X gives a critical analysis of Solzhenitsyn's work as compared with Tolstoy and Dostoevsky. Solzhenitsyn is also compared with prominent American authors such as Hemingway and Dos Passos.

3. The relationship of Solzhenitsyn to Stalin, Khrushchev, and present-day Russian political leaders is treated. Interesting accounts of Stalin's life and religious attitudes are given. The difference between the Socialist Realism of Russian leaders and Critical Realism of Solzhenitsyn is helpful. Insights given throw light on present-day disarmament talks.

4. Helpful insights are given regarding the Marxist-Leninist philosophy and its antecedents. Solzhenitsyn's evaluation of this philosophy is meaningful in today's world.

5. Summaries of Solzhenitsyn's chief works such as *The First Circle*, *One Day*, *The Gulag Archipelago*, and *Cancer Ward* are woven into the material in a skillful manner. Chapter IX provides an especially graphic summary of *The Gulag Archipelago*. The horror of prison life is dramatically portrayed.

6. The perspective of Solzhenitsyn on the Western Enlightenment and its relevance for Russia is evaluated. For Solzhenitsyn, a strong religious and theological base is necessary for freedom, equality, and brotherhood. Solzhenitsyn is presented as a man with strong Christian convictions.

7. Especially helpful is the description of the history of the Russian Orthodox Church. This development is seen

in the context of the total Christian and Islamic heritage with some interesting comparisons with Augustine. This material alone makes the book a "must."

8. Illuminating sections deal with Solzhenitsyn's perspective on basic Christian theological themes such as evil, suffering, free will, predestination, creation, and redemption. These doctrines come alive in the context of the dramatic events of Solzhenitsyn's life.

9. Noteworthy is Professor Nielsen's skillful use of particular places and landmarks in Russia. For example, Chapter VIII is introduced with a description of Leningrad's Museum of the History of Religion and Atheism. From this springboard, an interesting discussion is given of the history of religious persecution and planned secularization in Russia. The dialogue of Solzhenitsyn with the new Patriarch of the Russian Orthodox Church in regard to compromise is carefully spelled out.

10. This is more than a descriptive book. The wise evaluations and critiques are quite valuable. The book makes a strong moral and spiritual impact. In the doldrums of America's post-Watergate era it should be especially helpful in terms of its challenge to moral courage and even sacrifice for the sake of truth and human freedom. The book gives perspective for American Christian leaders and laypersons. Professor Nielsen presents Solzhenitsyn as a person who sees Christianity as a religion—not of escapism —but of ethical power. Solzhenitsyn's reaction to the "Big Lie" of the Stalin regime is dramatically portrayed. Suggestions for a patriotism tempered by theological, transnational, and ethical guidelines are helpful and relevant.

This is a timely book. Moreover, it is an *urgently needed* book. The writer of this Preface predicts its appeal will be widespread.

JOHN P. NEWPORT

CHAPTER I

The Making of an Author—
Solzhenitsyn's Rise from Obscurity

What kind of man is Alexander Solzhenitsyn? Prophet? Conspirator? Dissident? Patriot? Believer? Today, Solzhenitsyn is an international figure. His every word is seized upon by the press. A Nobel Prize winner, he commands a worldwide audience. All kinds of persons read his books. The United States has made him an "honorary citizen"; Billy Graham is quoted as saying that Solzhenitsyn "has the kind of intellect and moral courage that the world so desperately needs today." Nor has forced exile silenced his voice even in his native land; his many-volumed *The Gulag Archipelago*—taped from Radio Liberty—circulates underground in a variety of versions at high prices in the USSR.

But it was not always so. In 1962, when Solzhenitsyn was catapulted into prominence suddenly and unannounced with the publication of *One Day in the Life of Ivan Denisovich*, the ordinary Russian reader knew nothing about the author—much less his religious ideas. What has brought Solzhenitsyn into his present prominence is his moral courage. He survived imprisonment in the work camp. He has been in and out of favor with the regime. But he has never surrendered to nor accepted the Communist party line. The integrity of his life and reflection is evident in the fact that he was neither trapped nor destroyed by his enemies. He is his own man. In this book, that integrity, that moral courage, will be examined in the light of his religious beliefs.

1

A Fresh Perspective

Solzhenitsyn's religion is not described in detail in any one of his novels or other writings. He has given no systematic account of his belief in God. Rather, he often seems to speak through one of his characters, expressing his own convictions in this voice. Each of his works, successively, has given new knowledge about his outlook. *The Gulag Archipelago* concludes with important personal information about his way to religious faith; its later volumes, still to be published, yet may supply more. It is evident that Solzhenitsyn accepts the tradition which has been dominant throughout the history of his nation, Russian Orthodoxy. He is not uncritical of the earlier mixture of nationalism and piety in the mythology of Tsardom. However, he believes that the basic alternative is between a materialistic and a more spiritual view of life. Since his exile, Solzhenitsyn has spoken directly to religious questions in a letter written to emigre Orthodox Bishops. It is clear that Christian faith is not just a cultural consideration for him. He has never bracketed belief in God in the Western "secular" manner. His writings bring a fresh perspective, one that cannot be explained simply in stereotyped categories.

The Authentic Background

The background of Solzhenitsyn's novels is explained in detail in his most recent best seller, *The Gulag Archipelago*. Solzhenitsyn researched this dramatically written record of imprisonment under Stalin with the help of a host of living survivors. In order to protect them, he withheld publication. However, he did send copies outside of Russia; they were to be released if he were killed by the authorities. The secret police finally located the one remaining copy of the manuscript in Russia which was not in Solzhenitsyn's hands. It had been entrusted to a Leningrad woman for safekeeping. After five days of interrogation without sleep, she finally broke down and disclosed its whereabouts. Released from custody, she committed suicide. Solzhenitsyn feared that the information of the book would be used against his friends and helpers as well as himself. He ordered its publication in the West, an action which accelerated plans for his exile.

Boris Pasternak in his *Sketch for an Autobiography* breaks off his narrative with the words, "to continue it would be immeasurably difficult. . . . One would have to talk in a manner which would grip the heart and make the hair stand on end." [1] *The Gulag Archipelago* does just this. It is not simply that Solzhenitsyn has provided new and massive details about the forced labor camps. His genius as a writer is that he breathes life into his data. As Milovan Djilas, the former confidant of Tito and author of *Conversations with Stalin*, remarks: "What is new in *The Gulag Archipelago* is its authenticity and the breath of death and irrationality that permeates it. As a writer Solzhenitsyn is at his best when he describes concrete situations and events. Therefore *The Gulag* is his best book. Only a few other writers have managed to combine history, reporting and reflection in this way, and the picture of Soviet reality that emerges from *The Gulag* is overwhelming and lasting." [2] G. F. Kennan, the former United States Ambassador to Russia, concludes that "the book achieves, in its massiveness, its fierce frankness, and its compelling detail, an authority no amount of counter-propaganda will ever be able to shake. . . . [It emerges] as the greatest and most powerful single indictment of a political regime ever to be levelled in modern times. . . . It is impossible to believe that this book can have anything less than a major effect on the Soviet regime." [3]

Solzhenitsyn's Personal History

It is not surprising that, in the face of police harassment, Solzhenitsyn has guarded the details of his personal life carefully. He gave only a brief biography when he received the Nobel Prize for Literature in 1970. Evidently enough, his early life story supplied materials for his later career as a novelist. Solzhenitsyn's ancestors were not wealthy land-owners as Communist propaganda has reported; of peasant stock, they were twice exiled for resisting the Tsars. His father, an officer in the First World War, left the land to attend a university. He was killed in a hunting accident in June, 1918, six months before the son's birth. Alexander Solzhenitsyn was born December 11, 1918, at Kislovdsk in the foothills of the Caucasus Mountains. Mother and son together finally buried the father's war medals in order to hide them from the Communists. She came from the old intelligentsia and continued to attend church although she was not unusually religious.

Belonging to the postwar generation, Solzhenitsyn was well-indoctrinated in Marxism and the Stalinist party line at school. Even as a boy, he joined the struggle for exis-tence, standing in line for goods at the stores. When the civil war between the Whites and the Reds had ended, he and his mother settled at Rostov on the Don in 1924. She took a position as a shorthand typist. Solzhenitsyn had an obvious talent for mathematics and physics, and when he had finished intermediate school, he received a Stalin schol-arship at the local university. His scientific training was to rescue his career on a number of occasions, but in his mind it was secondary to the interest in writing which had come to occupy him at an unusually young age. Solzhenitsyn's critical judgment had already begun to develop.

Stalin's Lies

Early in life, Solzhenitsyn came to disbelieve Stalin's lies. Gleb Nerzhin in *The First Circle* reflects the "Emperor's New Clothes" psychology which Solzhenitsyn had devel-oped in what is clearly an autobiographical passage.

Gleb, at twelve, has read in *Izvestiya* of the trial of the saboteur engineers and cannot bring himself to believe in the truth of the accounts, voluminous though they are. He *knows* the trial is a lie. Then, as a ninth-grader, he sees in a display window the newspaper that tells of Kirov's death.

Intuitively he realizes that Stalin has killed Kirov. The knowledge creates a feeling of alienation in him, and he cannot understand why the grown men around him have not seen the same truth as he. To underscore the point, Solzhenitsyn, without a break, immediately shifts to the self-confessions of the Old Bolsheviks. Gleb is obviously Solzhenitsyn, and his lonely pain is Solzhenitsyn's pain.[4]

Resolving to educate himself in literature as well as science, in 1939 Solzhenitsyn enrolled in a two-year correspondence course at the Institute of History, Philosophy, and Literature in Moscow. He continued to study science and received his licentiate in mathematics and physics a few days before Hitler's attack on Russia. He was drafted on October 18, 1941. Married a year earlier, he was to be separated from his wife for more than a decade and a half.

For reasons of health, Solzhenitsyn, the soldier, was first assigned to drive transport wagons after the outbreak of the war. He worked with horses in this menial capacity until the spring of 1942.

Gleb Nerzhin in *The First Circle* repeats Solzhenitsyn's experience. He is at first clumsy and the butt of laughter, but he works himself up to the rank of artillery officer at which he is competent and happy.[5]

Although patriotic and engaged in battle by his own wish, Solzhenitsyn was not insensitive to the propaganda and brutality of the time. It was criticism of Stalin which led to his imprisonment in the concluding days of the Second World War. His assignment as an artillery officer took him all the way from Leningrad to East Prussia. Reaching the rank of captain, he received the Order of the Red Star for his bravery. Millions of Russian soldiers were imprisoned in the latter days of the war simply because they had been taken prisoner by the Germans and then returned to Russia. Solzhenitsyn was not among them. Contrary to rumors spread by his enemies, he was never captured. His rehabilitation protocol states that he corresponded with a friend who had been transferred to the Northern Front, N.D.

Vitkevich. Together, they criticized Stalin's military strategy and even his grammar. Solzhenitsyn also rejected the unreal atmosphere of many contemporary literary works which eulogized Stalin uncritically. He believed that "the Boss," as the Dictator was called in his letters, had betrayed Lenin's ideals and was responsible for the blunders which led to the disastrous loss of large areas of Russian territory in the opening struggle of the Second World War. This nickname used for Stalin was identified by SMERSH, the army counter-espionage organization whose title means, "death for spies." Solzhenitsyn's arrest during the siege of Konigsberg in East Germany was delayed because he was still in battle. Stripped of his decorations and emblems of rank, he was taken to Lubyanka prison in Moscow and processed in the manner described at the end of his novel, *The First Circle*. The first hours of the prisoner, Solzhenitsyn, were the basis for his description of his character Innokenty.

Innokenty is subjected to a dehumanizing and degrading physical examination by the warder. He had expected a tense clash of wits; he finds he is treated as an animal.[6]

A sentence of eight years forced labor plus three years exile was imposed by judges who did not confront Solzhenitsyn personally. The guards told Solzhenitsyn, the prisoner, that he was no more than an insect. This is the term Lenin had applied to "class enemies." Solzhenitsyn pictures Ahmadjan, one of Beria's boys, saying of the zeks, "They no human beings." As his belief in Marxist ideology was shattered, the possibility of religious meaning grew ever larger in Solzhenitsyn's consciousness. Sheer physical vitality, of which he exhibited remarkably much, was not enough to sustain him in prison. Solzhenitsyn's experience as a prisoner gave clear evidence at one point. Men who believe only in themselves fall victims of their captors and are destroyed. Theoretical as well as practical questions persisted in his consciousness. Solzhenitsyn could not believe that history is the last word as the Communist party claimed; if so, it would be a despairing one for him. Working as a prisoner with other scientists, he saw how scientific discovery can be bent to perverse ends, destructive of man's humanity.

Solzhenitsyn was assigned as a "zek" to a building project in Moscow. In *The First Circle*, Gleb Nerzhin helps build an MVD apartment house. Is Nerzhin's pride of workmanship also Solzhenitsyn's? [7]

Subsequently, Solzhenitsyn's mathematical training rescued his career again. He had to fill out an "efficiency form" which disclosed his background. Thanks to this document he was assigned to a scientific institute at Mavrino in the outskirts of Moscow. A year later he was transferred to "the lowest circle of hell," the labor camp at Ekibastuz. Set in the semidesert of Central Asia, the camp belonged to the Gulag Archipelago and was as large as France. Prisoners wore numbers on their chest, back, and one knee. Following Stalin's death, Solzhenitsyn was released to spend the rest of his life in "eternal" exile; in 1953 he was forbidden ever to return to European Russia. Living in a mud hut in the village of Kok-Terek southwest of Lake Balkhash, he secured a position teaching mathematics and physics at a lower school. Solzhenitsyn had had an operation for an abdominal cancer before he left the work camp. Although it reappeared and caused great pain, it was some time before the local NKVD commander gave permission for him to go to the hospital at Tashkent, the capital of Uzbekistan where his life was saved by radiation. In fact, he was a freak medical case. The cells of his body were not damaged by x-rays. His body could take unusually large doses which would have killed other persons. Bethell explains.

> The growth of his belly made it impossible for him to sit up and made him think of nothing but pain. . . . In the hospital he was given massive irradiation and injections, and in three days was a human being again. The

cancer is still there, a solid lump, but it seldom bothers him and is not something his friends worry about.[8]

Following a review of his case in 1956, he was able to move in June of that year to Ryazan, 280 miles from Moscow. Reunited with his wife, he continued as a school teacher, but gave more and more time to his writing. He kept it secret from everyone except her until 1961. Then, in the era of growing destalinization, he finally took courage and sent a manuscript to the literary journal *Novy Mir* in Moscow.

"A New Classic"

Tvardovsky, the editor, later recounted the impression that Solzhenitsyn's novella made upon him. He had gone home for the evening and was following his usual routine of undressing, going to bed, and lighting a cigar. Then, he took from his pile of manuscripts a copy of *One Day in the Life of Ivan Denisovich*, sent by Alexander Solzhenitsyn from Ryazan, and began to read. Tvardovsky records:

> I realized at once that here was something important, and that in some way I must celebrate the event. I got out of bed, got fully dressed again in every particular, and sat down at my desk. That night I read a new classic of Russian literature.

Tvardovsky was impressed not only by the manuscript's utterly convincing truthfulness but also its warmth of style. He recognized that it had a unique quality, as it treated themes long suppressed in Russian literature during the Communist era: tyranny and injustice, suffering, evil, and death. Tvardovsky contacted Premier Khrushchev who himself read the manuscript and made its publication part of his campaign of destalinization. The first edition was sold out almost immediately on the newsstands as soon as it appeared in print. Countless families who had had members imprisoned in the Stalin era recognized their own story.

Khrushchev and Solzhenitsyn

After the publication of *One Day*, Solzhenitsyn, now a celebrity, was invited to a reception which Khrushchev gave for the leaders of Soviet arts and letters. The direction of his policies was not altogether clear. It is reported that some of the guests wore dark suits; others chose only to come in business dress. Still others were in old style Stalin tunics, as the Premier's attitude toward the Dictator had become less overtly hostile. Solzhenitsyn's suit was described in the words of an old Russian saying, as hanging on him as if chewed by a cow. His dress stood out from the crowd so much as to evoke questions about why he had been invited. Khrushchev himself led an ovation for Solzhenitsyn. Surrounded by a group of his guests, he announced, "Comrades, Solzhenitsyn is among us." Raising his hands, he applauded. Solzhenitsyn is reported to have shown little visible reaction to the honor that he was given. He retained a kind of "prisoner's mask" born of long experience. His face remained stern, his eyes blank. The fact was that liberalization and reform had already begun to be arrested by Khrushchev's fellow Politburo members in the Kremlin. Burg and Feifer hold that within a week of *One Day's* appearance the tide of destalinization had turned.

Solzhenitsyn's prayer to God dates from this period:

How easy it is for me to live with you, Lord!
How easy for me to believe in you.
When my spirit is lost, perplexed and cast down,
When the sharpest can see no further than the night,
And know not what on the morrow they must do
You give me a sure certainty
That you exist, that you are watching over me
And will not permit the ways of righteousness to be closed
  to me.
Here on the summit of earthly glory I look back aston-
  ished

On the road which through depths of despair has led me
here.
To this point from which I can also reflect to men your
radiance
And all that I can still reflect—you shall grant to me.
And what I shall fail you shall grant to others.[9]

Solzhenitsyn's life has spanned an era of almost bound-
less cruelty in which religion has been persecuted by
fascists and Communists alike. Born after the revolution,
he does not look back in archaism to an older and better
age. His protest is a genuinely contemporary one. Solzhenitsyn's conviction is that Stalin's atheism corrupted the
political order. Meaningless utopian certainties were proclaimed by a revolutionary ideology which denies the existence of God. Long-standing assurances of justice, order,
and personal worth dissolved for countless millions of victims under Communist rule. In the end, propaganda and
class justice did not bring moral reform but only the perennial brutality of tyranny in even more vast and terrible
form.

Solzhenitsyn had no need to conjure up a straw man as the
embodiment of tyranny. The evil he rejects was summed
up in the person of the Dictator whom he hates so intensely. Solzhenitsyn's *The Gulag Archipelago* saw the result of Stalin's atheism as sixty-six million casualties for the
new order in Russia alone. The tyrant shaped both the
ideology and political structures of an era, simplifying what
Marx and Lenin had taught, even as he continued in their
anti-religious tradition.

In *Stories and Prose Poems*, Solzhenitsyn symbolizes
Russia as a secret lake in a secret forest enslaved by an evil
prince.[10] The evil prince is Stalin, but this is not all
that Solzhenitsyn is trying to say. The Communist revolution has failed in its promise to him and his fellow prisoners.
Rejection of its ideology is necessary to integrity. Solzhenitsyn does not believe that trust in God is only an opiate of
the people as Marx declared. For him, personal Providence

has become a living reality. His way to this knowledge was through the degradation and inhumanity of totalitarian imprisonment. It is a mistake to suppose that he retreated to religion simply in weakness. His sane healthy-mindedness, even more apparent after his exile to the West than before, remained with him. The abiding optimism, reflected throughout his novels, has sustained his resistance to tyranny. Yet for him evil is not just an idea, but practically efficacious.

A Matter of Conscience

Solzhenitsyn's writing, from the beginning, has been motivated by a sense of duty to the millions of innocent victims who perished under Stalin's terror. It is a matter of conscience for him that the experience of the work camps shall not be forgotten. He does not speak merely theoretically against injustice, but out of what he has endured. Writers in the West sometimes have to resort to fantasy when they write realism. Solzhenitsyn does not. Solzhenitsyn's first-hand knowledge and candor evoke sympathy from his audience together with a suspension of disbelief. Jacobson comments:

> Solzhenitsyn takes for granted an absolutely direct and open connection between literature and morality, art and life. He believes our responsibilities in the one to be inseparable from our responsibilities in the other; indeed, to be all but identical with one another.
> In the West today such an assumption about the relationship between art and morality is distinctly unfashionable. We like to insist nowadays on the detachment of art from moral considerations. . . . Or if we admit any commerce between art and morality . . . what we are likely to demand of our art is that it should subvert and overthrow all the traditional moral notions; that it should do its best to fragment the self into a thousand pieces, rather than to stress its organic wholeness.[11]

It is not to be denied that Solzhenitsyn uses extreme and marginal settings. The era has been one in which the extraordinary seems ordinary and the ordinary extraordinary. Rothberg points out that Solzhenitsyn's use of "they" of the rulers and "we" of the ruled has a long usage in Russian literary tradition. Solzhenitsyn's primary commitment is to the worth of the human individual, and he insists that persons cannot surrender their freedom. He is convinced that men are individually responsible for their societies. Evil societies breed evil men, but evil men also make evil societies. The gulf between Marxism's words and deeds, its promises and achievements, shocked Solzhenitsyn out of complacency.

Solzhenitsyn's intention is to take the scales from the eyes of his reader. This can be seen in his play, *The Love Girl and the Innocent*, for example.

There is a "second curtain" between the audience and the play, and this second curtain is crudely posterized with all the stock elements of Soviet propaganda: happy industry, cheerful workers, and a benevolent Stalin.[12]

Behind the second curtain, the viewer sees prisoners, guards, barbed wire, and the watchtowers of a concentration camp. Persons with decency and a sense of values are perennially under attack in Solzhenitsyn's stories. Their very existence makes the immorality and cruelty of the system in which they live doubly apparent. Courage accounts for much of Solzhenitsyn's role of leadership as a literary hero. The police were not able to cow him into submission or to destroy him directly and so exiled him.

Solzhenitsyn's Literary Technique

Solzhenitsyn's social criticism uses tools from the modern literary tradition. His experience is too contemporary to allow him to be labeled simply. His historical novel, *August 1914*, borrows techniques learned from the American writer, John Dos Passos. He is also indebted to Ernest Hemingway whom he commends for terseness of style, frankness, and contempt for falsehood, although Solzhenitsyn does not admire him greatly. Solzhenitsyn does not compose novels with conventional main characters and minor characters, plots and subplots. More modernistically, he employs a series of interrelated episodes which are united by ideological content as well as story. His many-sided and polyphonic novels have no single hero, although some characters are more developed than others. He gives no neat answer, but instead raises questions. It was noted at the Nobel Prize Festival which he could not attend that the total reaction of his characters alone expresses the full breadth of his moral and social vision.

For Solzhenitsyn even as a youth, Stalinism made doubly clear that the dignity of the human person can no longer be taken for granted. Not just churchmen, but old Bolsheviks, peasants and workers were annihilated. At the same time, the tie between liberty of conscience and belief in God became ever more evident. Modern totalitarianism has attempted to crush the two together, seeking to control the life of man completely.

Defender of Human Dignity

Self-consciously, Solzhenitsyn has become a defender of human dignity as well as conscience. He is outspoken against any lasting break between the political and the ethical. In his Nobel Prize lecture, he argues that the writer is to create for mankind one system of interpretation, valid for good and evil deeds, for the unbearable and bearable, as they are differentiated today. Through a work of literature, the reader is released from his numbness to the events of public life. He is not simply a spectator any longer. Solzhenitsyn offers perspective on contemporary life in his fusion of history and fiction. He fictionalizes history and historicizes fiction. The single-dimension objectivity of a media-dominated age is seen as illusory; reality is many-sided. Solzhenitsyn's writing fills part of the void left by historians and journalists who have degenerated into spokesmen for Communist repression. It even assumes some of the role of religious leadership which has been defaulted by the submission of the established Church to an atheistic regime. Questions of a particular political system, east or west although not unimportant, are secondary. Most fundamental is right and wrong, the ethical bases necessary for community. In his Nobel Prize lecture, Solzhenitsyn warned:

> Let us not forget that violence does not and cannot exist by itself; it is invariably intertwined with *the lie.* They are linked in the most intimate, most organic and profound fashion: violence cannot conceal itself behind anything except lies, and lies have nothing to maintain them save violence. Anyone who has once proclaimed violence as his method must inexorably choose the lie as his principle.[13]

David Halperin points out that Solzhenitsyn is familiar with the description of the devil in the words ascribed to Jesus by John 8:44. "When he speaketh a lie, he speaketh of his own; for he is a liar, and the father of it." Solzhenitsyn invokes this Scripture against Stalin. The Dictator in himself is responsible for the omnipresent use of lying to the point of metaphysical deception. Untruth is willed by Stalin himself who lives completely in the world of lies he has engendered. From the Dictator's point of view, Solzhenitsyn was a conspirator against him.

Levels of Lying

Halperin finds three levels of falsehood depicted in Solzhenitsyn's novels: the empirical, psychological, and metaphysical.[14] The empirical lie he depicts by facts and occurrences; the psychological he portrays in personalities and actions; and the metaphysical he represents in symbols and ideas. Empirical falsehood—the most obvious—is typified by misleading newspaper reporting, altered production statistics, and blatant propaganda. Psychological, pragmatic lies produce warped codes of moral conduct which undermine the individual's ethical system. Metaphysical lies can deform the general world view of individuals or an entire nation, corrupting their value systems and modes of thought.

The Creativity of Solzhenitsyn

Not every author who has the courage to defy the regime turns out to be a great writer, much less a responsible interpreter of history. Solzhenitsyn has combined social concern with intense creativity. Lucid remarks that he is the artist descended from the ivory tower and attempting to extend his influence to the control tower of society. But Solzhenitsyn was never isolated above the multitude. It is not just Communism which is the enemy. The danger is that the writer's work will become a piece of merchandise to be consumed in the market place. This is especially the case in an era of mass media. Modern technology and industrialism have led to a one-dimensional type of man. Bureaucracies attempt to organize, manipulate, and encompass every element of man's being by technological reason. Solzhenitsyn recognizes that modern conditions too easily result in impersonalism. Community breaks down. Individuals are not able to react politically or even humanly to events. Solzhenitsyn believes that in such a situation the mission of the writer is doubly clear. Renouncing any Tolstoy-like retreat into innerliness, he joins thought and action as prophet.

Solzhenitsyn, having opened up an area for discussion formerly off bounds, has steadfastly refused to remove himself from public life and become a simply private author. Had he done this, he would soon have become again a nameless, faceless figure. He would have been a prisoner whether in or out of a prison camp. He is not a hermit type, even though he was forced into a kind of "Kafkaesque" loneliness before his exile from Russia. As social critic, Solzhenitsyn seeks a dialogue about destiny and righteousness with his reader. It is not too much to say that he joins his own quest for salvation with that of his nation. Litera-

ture is for him a way to human freedom. It is at this point
that his writings have political and religious implications.
He seeks to fashion an image from the national memory,
reviving the ancient role of the artist as a source of community symbols and beliefs. Marxism along with other
Western ideologies has produced institutionalized despotism. Solzhenitsyn believes that only an indigenous spiritual force can counter the nature of the present and past
regimes. In his public role, Solzhenitsyn even takes on
something of the function of tribal truth-teller and sooth-
sayer. He still wishes to make sense of the nation's destiny
and discover an alternative to an unbroken succession of
despotism.

Amid the Prison Camp Regime— Solzhenitsyn's First Novel, *One Day in the Life of Ivan Denisovich*

Terrance Des Pres emphasizes that violence has been total and impersonal in the twentieth century.[1] There is no longer any rational or affective relation between victim and aggressor. Human destruction has been en masse.

Solzhenitsyn's books, however, are an inventory of the victimization of innocence. Whereas Dostoevsky's criminals have sinned against other persons, Solzhenitsyn's victims end up in camps because they are innocent. Often, it is because they have refused to condone evil that they are imprisoned. Defying the all-powerful state, the prisoner seeks to keep a living soul in a living body.

What Solzhenitsyn has to say is best understood by beginning with his first book, the short novel *One Day in the Life of Ivan Denisovich* (1962). This anguished protest against the turning of the Soviet Union into a prison camp regime by Stalin and the other betrayers of the Revolution has implicit within it most of the major themes of his writings.

Solzhenitsyn's protest is not unrelated to his religious faith. He will not deny that he trusts in God. Burg and Feifer point out that as early as 1962, even as he was applauded by Khrushchev, Solzhenitsyn had come to a positive affirmation that he would not have made when he was released from imprisonment.[2] To be sure, he does speak of the impression which attendance at worship left on him as

17

a child. In the camps, he had witnessed the purity of life of
believers.

Solzhenitsyn could not reduce persons to things, good
and evil to expedience. In his imprisonment, he became
more than ever conscious of an inner struggle for righteousness and selfhood. Both have their being from God. "Is the
end of life happiness?" he asked. It is too much to expect
that men can live always without it. Yet it seems to belong
to animals as they devour their prey as well as to humans.
More uniquely human are sympathy, communication, and
love. These presuppose not just a historical cause or ideology but a person whose dignity and freedom must be
recognized.

Every bit of Solzhenitsyn's moral insight and perspective
on himself has been won personally against an oppressive
ideology. Communist materialism allows no absolute apart
from the present world; no price is too high for the survival
of the Party. Against such perversion, Solzhenitsyn is prepared to fight and die.

The Meaning of Humanity

For Solzhenitsyn, every person, in or out of prison, must
ask what it means to be a human being. He appeals to the
longer tradition of Russian social criticism against a shal-
low understanding of revolution. Tolstoy appears as a character in one of the opening chapters of his historical novel,
August 1914. His *What Men Live By* circulates in the
cancer ward. Solzhenitsyn has learned much from him as a
writer and admires the Tolstoyian virtues of love of neighbor, humility, family loyalty, compassion, and pity. However, Solzhenitsyn finds them insufficient in the face of the
cruelty and evil in the world of today. Thus it is a mistake
to regard Solzhenitsyn as a twentieth-century representa-
tive of this conviction. His outlook and stance preclude non-
reaction. Lucid points out that the prison camps as Solzhenitsyn describes them are a total institution set within
a larger society which is also a total institution. Outside

the camps as much as in them, Soviet officials twist the law as they wish. The problem is not just the demands of the situation, but how to retain integrity. The authentic artist must write what he actually observes and experiences, exposing the falsehood used to justify social evil.[3]

Ivan Denisovich Shukhov is the chief character of the story which suddenly brought Solzhenitsyn to fame in the Khrushchev era of destalinization. Prisoner 854, he is in the eighth year of his sentence. Ivan was captured in the war by the Germans, escaped to his own lines, and was charged with treason. His fate is typical of millions of others. Solzhenitsyn has remarked that "of all the drama that Russia lived through, the fate of Ivan Denisovich was the greatest tragedy." [4]

Solzhenitsyn has Shukhov tell his story from a limited but eyewitness point of view. There is a first person effect even in much of his descriptive narrative. Solzhenitsyn does not build up his character or the story with an accumulation of minute detail in the manner of Tolstoy. Nor does he express indignation or make polemical statements in the style of Dostoevsky. *One Day in the Life of Ivan Denisovich* is without the generalizations or even the overview which Dostoevsky gave to the same theme a hundred years earlier. It is argued that the characters of *One Day* lack psychological complexity. Yet Solzhenitsyn does make clear the organic wholeness of goodness even in simplicity and shows its monstrous antithesis in evil.

A Microcosm of Russia

Solzhenitsyn's intention is explicit. "It is not the task of the writer to defend or criticize one or another mode of distributing the social product or to defend one or another form of government organization. The task of the writer is to select more universal, eternal questions (such as) the secrets of the human heart, the triumph over spiritual sorrow, the laws of the history of mankind that were born in the depths of time immemorial and that will cease to exist only when the sun ceases to shine." [5] The prison camp is a microcosm of life in Russia. Although people in the camps are worse off than those in the country at large, the spectre of terror and blackmail stretches throughout Russian society. Its inmates are Russian, Ukranian, Estonian, Latvian, and even gypsy in background. Tiurin, son of a rich kulak, has spent more than twenty years in the camps for concealing his origin. Buinovsky, a former naval officer remains a confirmed Communist. He was imprisoned when he received a gift from a British officer with whom he was assigned to liaison during the war. There is Volkovoi, a former lieutenant in the security police, and Fetiukov, who was a government bureaucrat. Tsezar, an intellectual, had been a film producer. Alyosha, a Baptist, was sentenced for his religious beliefs.

Solzhenitsyn cites Tolstoy's comment that a novel can deal with either centuries of European history or one day of a man's life; in writing of Shukhov, he chose the latter. George Lukacs, the Hungarian Communist, has commented: "Solzhenitsyn's achievement consists in the literary transformations of the uneventful day in a typical camp into a symbol of a past which has not yet been overcome, nor has it been portrayed artistically. Although the camps epitomize one extreme of the Stalin era, the author has made his skillful grey monochrome of camp life into a symbol of everyday life under Stalin. He was successful in this precisely because he posed the artistic question: What demands has this era made on man? Who has proved himself a human being? Who has salvaged his human dignity and integrity? Who has held his own—and how? Who has retained his essential humanity? Where was his humanity twisted and destroyed? His rigorous limitation to the immediate camp life permits Solzhenitsyn to pose the question simultaneously in quite general and quite concrete terms." [6]

Solzhenitsyn's story treats a single day in January, 1951, when the 104th squad of prisoners, *zeks*, has been assigned to build a wall. The icy grip of winter is evident everywhere. Ivan's squad leader must keep his group from being sent to the "Socialist Way of Life," a site on the bare frozen steppe where there is no place for the prisoners to get warm, and many will die. Solzhenitsyn uses the camp to show the dishonesty and corruption of Soviet society at large. Work reports are fabricated en masse. Prisoners are stripped for searching in the cold. When Buinovsky, the former naval commander, complains that this is against socialist legality, he is thrown into solitary confinement for ten days.

One of the worst features of the camps is that criminals and political offenders are mixed together promiscuously. Stalin designated the former as "social allies" and the latter as "social enemies." Even in such circumstances work does give some solace. At the end of his day, Ivan finds satisfaction in having built a straight wall. The accomplishment of a good day's work affirms his worth and manliness. Lakshin comments: "Were Solzhenitsyn an artist of smaller scale and less sensitivity, he would probably have selected the worst day in the most arduous period of Ivan Denisovich's camp life. But he took a different road, one possible only for a writer who is certain of his own strength, who realizes that the subject of his story is of such importance and gravity that it excludes empty sensationalism and the desire to shock with descriptions of suffering and physical pain. Thus, by placing himself in apparently the most difficult and disadvantageous circumstances before the reader, who in no way expects to encounter a 'happy' day in the convicts' life, the author thereby ensured the full objectivity of his artistic testimony, and all the more mercilessly and sharply struck a blow at the crimes of the recent past." [7]

Three Types of Religion
Rothberg points out that there are three types of religion in *One Day*. Alyosha is a Baptist Christian.[8] Buinovsky retains his Communist idealism. Tsezar's commitment is to

the art of the cinema. The camp is a place of Christian testing for Alyosha. He tells Ivan: "That's why your prayers
stay unanswered. One must never stop praying. If you
have real faith you tell a mountain to move and it will
move." [9] One should not pray for any material or mortal
thing, except for "our daily bread," and one ought not even
to pray to be freed from the camp: "Why do you want
freedom? In freedom your last grain of faith will be choked
with weeds. You should rejoice that you're in prison. Here
you have time to think about your soul." Ivan replies to
Alyosha: "Jesus Christ wanted you to sit in prison and so
you are—sitting there for His sake. But for whose sake am
I here? Because we weren't ready for war in forty-one? For
that? But was that *my* fault?" Alyosha's eyes glow like
candles, and he tries to persuade Ivan Denisovich to let his
soul pray. However, he receives the reply: "Prayers are like
those appeals of ours. Either they don't get through or
they're returned with 'rejected' scrawled across 'em." But
Ivan does believe in God and at the end of the day prays:
"Glory be to Thee, O Lord. Another day over. Thank You
I'm not spending tonight in the cells. Here it's still bearable." Ivan cannot understand why Alyosha should have
been sentenced to twenty-five years for his faith in God. He
was a man who, even in imprisonment, could be relied on
not to squeal, and was happy. "What had he to be happy
about? His cheeks were sunken, he lived strictly on his
rations, he earned nothing. He spent all his Sundays mut-
tering with the other Baptists. They shed the hardships of
camp life like water off a duck's back." "You could count on
Alyosha. Did whatever was asked of him. If everybody in
the world was like that, Shukhov would have done likewise.
If a man asks for help why not help him? Those Baptists
had something there."

Tiurin, Ivan's "steel-chested" squad leader, was thrown
out of the army by his commander, because he was the son
of a kulak. He meets the officer again and learns that his
former superior has been sentenced to ten years. Tiurin,

too, believes in God. "The regimental commander and the commissar," Tiurin recounts, "were both shot in thirty-seven, no matter whether they were of proletarian or kulak stock, whether they had a conscience or not. So I crossed myself and said: 'So, after all, Creator, You do exist up there in heaven. Your patience is long-suffering but You strike hard.' " [10] Shukhov respects the Communist idealism of Buinovsky, the former naval commander; he not only has scientific knowledge but also is committed to socialist justice. Yet the peasant senses that he has not yet learned the lessons of survival in the camps. Solzhenitsyn shows Shukhov bringing Tsezar his supper, a bowl of cold buckwheat mush. Tsezar has just received a package, and Shukhov hopes that he will refuse the mush and leave it for its bearer to eat. Although Tsezar's ultimate commitment is to art, he expresses Solzhenitsyn's own judgment. "Ham," said X 123 angrily. . . . "It's all so arty there's no art left in it. Spice and poppyseed instead of everyday bread and butter! And then, the vicious political idea—the justification of personal tyranny. A mockery of the memory of three generations of Russian intelligentsia. . . . Geniuses don't adjust their interpretations to suit the taste of tyrants!" [11]

The majority of prisoners, like Ivan, are Reds. Solzhenitsyn makes clear that Ivan's humanity helps him to stay alive. The Blacks, those who start revolts, perish. His strategy is survival, but not at any price. Solzhenitsyn portrays Ivan Denisovich Shukhov as a hardworking, shrewd, and sensible peasant. He can be cunning when necessary but is not vicious or violent. Responsible and compassionate yet ignorant, he will help a fellow prisoner when requested. His ethics and religion are his family; his goal, release.

> Shukhov . . . didn't know whether he wanted freedom or not. At first he had longed for it. Every day he'd counted the days of his stretch—how many had passed, how many were coming. And then he'd grown bored with counting. And then it became clear that men of his like wouldn't

ever be allowed to return home, and they'd be exiled. And whether his life would be any better there than here—who could tell? Freedom meant one thing to him—home. But they wouldn't let him go home.[12] Other writers, Communist and non-Communist, have given much darker pictures of the camps. Prisoners beg for death. They are told that they are nothing and reduced to nothing. Doctors commit suicide. Solzhenitsyn's writing by its sober documentary tone avoids overdone rhetoric.

The dramatic impact which Solzhenitsyn's first book, *One Day in the Life of Ivan Denisovich*, had on the Russian reading public can hardly be overstated. It was privately duplicated even before its publication, although there were drastic rules against such practice at the publishing house.[13] In the end, though, Solzhenitsyn evoked outspoken hatred as well as admiration. His enemies depicted him as locked in the stifling atmosphere of the nineteenth century. His pessimistic, mystical world view, they said, precludes him from comprehending reality in its revolutionary development. The letters which circulated underground as *samizdat* put it otherwise: "What were our homegrown bosses thinking of, shutting Solzhenitsyn's mouth . . . ?" I pity those readers who do not know that there is a great Russian writer living and working in the land of Russia. . . ." Solzhenitsyn in his Nobel lecture was to remark: "Contemporary science knows that suppression of information leads to entropy and universal destruction." [14]

Georg Lukacs, the longtime Hungarian literary critic and Communist, was singularly impressed with *One Day in the Life of Ivan Denisovich*. Lukacs hailed it as the proper fruit of socialist realism. Shortly before his death, Lukacs drew a parallel between Thomas Mann's *The Magic Mountain* and Solzhenitsyn's novels. He found in both an expansion of a novella to a larger, but concentrated setting. Solzhenitsyn continues the tradition of the epoch novel. In this sense he is nineteenth century and follows Tolstoy. He also reflects Tolstoy's moral earnestness. Yet Lukacs found *One Day* too plebian, to be sure, unmarxist. The dialectic between the individual and the group had broken down. However, he apparently admired the fact that Solzhenitsyn was not always looking back over his shoulder, seeking to discern what Communist Party officials wished. Solzhenitsyn refused all distortion of truth and reality opposed to his conscience; it can lead only to a literature which is vapid, lifeless, and inane. In short, Solzhenitsyn refused to be ideologically orthodox. He was and remains a realist! [An excellent discussion of the critical response to Solzhenitsyn may be found in *Aleksandr Solzhenitsyn: Critical Essays and Documentary Materials*, edited by John B. Dunlop, Richard Haugh, and Alexis Klimoff, Nordland, 1973.]

The Road to Christianity

Solzhenitsyn in his Nobel Prize speech proclaimed "his complete disagreement with the age which believes that there are no stable and universal concepts of justice and good, that all values are fluid, that they change." [15] This fundamental conviction, assuredly, led him on to Christianity. Many men, East and West, would deny Solzhenitsyn's view; but confronted by totalitarian oppression, in and out of the prison camps, he remains unimpressed. Nihilism is no answer to despair!

Before Solzhenitsyn's writings had been forced into underground circulation, they had made their impact, and he had emerged as the leading Russian writer of the era—linked to a great tradition. Solzhenitsyn's novels are not religious in the obvious sense. They develop no explicitly Christian notions overtly. His achievement is one of realism—Russian realism as against socialist realism. Solzhenitsyn's moral courage has been that he will not be silenced. This moral courage is reinforced by the profundity and skill with which he explains his ideas. Solzhenitsyn's Christian faith is to be explained intellectually from the fact that he had come to feel the need for the steady presence of a

powerful good which would take him through suffering giving perspective; human beings should not be taken up
simply with the part, he concluded.

But With This Reservation

Although he has been outspoken against the persecutors
of the Church, Solzhenitsyn has not allowed himself to become an apologist. Believers in God receive no more sym-
pathetic treatment than others of his characters. Christian
commitment does not prejudice his telling observations of
people or social conditions.

CHAPTER III

Critics and Enemies— The Nobel Prize Winner Is Rejected in Russia

Solzhenitsyn has remarked, "You know, I would prefer to be published widely in my own country." [1] Paradoxically, his fame has grown in Russia at the same time that he has become known abroad. He acknowledges that the world-wide community of writers has had a major role in preserving his life. Solzhenitsyn's strategy has been almost the exact opposite of that of Boris Pasternak. Pasternak had hoped to take advantage of an earlier thaw to publish his novel, *Doctor Zhivago*, in 1955. Of a drastically different disposition than Solzhenitsyn, he shunned public life. Attacked personally, Pasternak not only renounced the Nobel Prize and his novel as well, but made a humiliating public confession of self-criticism. In principle, he had wished to maintain internal independence and live apart from Communist ideology. Before his death, Pasternak remarked that *Doctor Zhivago* was a "victim of the cold war." [2] Every country has its quotas of such men. The universality of his novel had been unfairly distorted. In fact, Pasternak met defeat because he could not combine spirituality with social involvement. Instead, he found spiritual life inimical to a public role. There was a kernel of truth in the Communist charge that he misjudged the political and social repercussions of his writing. Still, as a Christian, he had violated the Marxist "socialist aesthetic" and retreated. In contrast, Solzhenitsyn has stood his ground.

Party Support for Solzhenitsyn

Solzhenitsyn was a complete unknown when Khrushchev endorsed his book in 1962. While he had this support, it could be said that his writings conformed to the Party line. Khrushchev had characterized Stalin as a "seriously sick man, suffering from suspiciousness and persecution mania" and revealed the Dictator's plan "to destroy a considerable part of the artistic intelligentsia of the Soviet Ukraine." The new leader said that he had pride in the Soviet creative intelligentsia and was ready to stand behind it. Socialist art should express "artistic and social truth, however harsh it may be." Although Khrushchev advocated a "realistic literature which described the common national experience," he did not sanction non-partisanship in the arts. He wished, with the help of such men as Tvardovsky, who discovered Solzhenitsyn, to develop a progressive public consciousness. Khrushchev's objection to abstract art was that it does not serve the needs and interest of the people. He explained:

> Soviet literature and art are called on to reproduce in bright artistic imagery the great heroic epoch of Communist construction and to depict truthfully the assertion and victory of new communist relations in our life. The artist must be able to see the positive things and to rejoice at them since they comprise the essence of our reality; he must support these things but meanwhile, of course, he must not overlook the negative aspects and all that interferes with the rise of what is new in life.[3]

Solzhenitsyn's writings were used by the "liberals" to further their cause during Khrushchev's relatively short-lived campaign of destalinization. Never the majority, this faction was defeated by the hardliners even before Khrushchev resigned.

Solzhenitsyn's Enemies

Solzhenitsyn has always had strong enemies as well as admirers. Half jokingly he remarked to a visitor, "I've been living off the mistake of Russia's last dictator." There seem to have been personal denunciations in Solzhenitsyn's secret police file at the time of his arrest. The police have continued to regard him as dangerous, in the end seeking to blunt his protest by exile. They were not able to prove any charges of dishonesty against Solzhenitsyn in their numerous searches and surveillance. In such circumstances, Solzhenitsyn was forced to guard his private life closely and would not give interviews even after he received the Nobel Prize. He did choose to speak with foreign correspondents on several occasions, attempting to use the fact that he was known outside of Russia for self-defense. Although not seeking conflict, Solzhenitsyn was not withdrawn from it. The pressures directed against him did not break him, but instead increased his determination. A month after his expulsion from the Writers' Union, Molotov was asked how Stalin would have dealt with him. The answer came without hesitation, "Solzhenitsyn would have been shot." [4]

Socialist Realism and Critical Realism

To understand Solzhenitsyn's cause, one must distinguish between *socialist realism* and *critical realism*. Stalin, defining *socialist realism* in 1932, insisted that writers portray the utopian Communist society of the future. They were to write only the "typical" and "uplifting." Of course, Solzhenitsyn and his friends attempted to break out of such banality in affirmation of an absolute justice; a man's actions cannot violate his conscience. For Stalin, the assertion of absolute moral norms independent of the regime and its dogmas was tantamount to treason. The fact is that Solzhenitsyn's *critical realism* does not conform to

Communist dogma as socialist realism. Solzhenitsyn presents alternative political and philosophical solutions; the norms of socialist realism are set entirely by the government. Solzhenitsyn by contrast expects the reader to make his own moral judgments as to whether he depicts life as it is actually experienced. At a meeting of the Secretariat of the Union of Soviet Writers in the fall of 1967, Riurikov, a writer, demanded that Solzhenitsyn renounce the title of "continuer of Russian realism." Solzhenitsyn answered: "Placing my hand on my heart, I swear that I shall never do it." [5]

Solzhenitsyn Versus Soviet Ideology Techniques

Soviet ideology uses slogans and clichés in stereotyped formulas to cover its own intentions. Solzhenitsyn protests that such propaganda is a fraud; only as it is rejected can the reader come to terms with political reality. Propaganda dehumanizes persons in abstraction. The artist must create language from within, searching for new forms of expression. He becomes ineffective if he clings to old lifeless and ready made forms. Solzhenitsyn regarded Stalin's comment that language is a tool of production as nonsense. Lucid points out that he wills to become a public symbol, capturing the attention and creating national feeling.[6] The images which he creates are intended to stir men's lives and effect change. He knows that an authentic artist can have a cathartic effect. Solzhenitsyn writes in populist and not mandarin style, using the jargon of the street or prison. Both stylistic and national norms are called into question by his work. Pushkin and Tolstoy, Solzhenitsyn urges, provided a counterforce to tyranny in their own times. They were effective when every other avenue of freedom was closed. Solzhenitsyn looks to their example. It is conscience which makes him a human being as well as part of the people. He will not retreat into a world of private fantasy in the face of repression. Solzhenitsyn will not live and create according to predefined standards of the Party but solely according to the standards of his own "inner self." He believes that when writers give up their mission, the world falls into the hands of madmen and mercenaries.

Karl Marx and the Role of the Artist

Marx early recognized the artist's capacity to shape the ethos of an era and to further social vision. The sensitive and discerning writer can be the eye, ear, and heart of culture. How was this conviction joined to Marx's materialism and economic determinism? Understanding the writer as an expression of the interests of an economic group, Communism necessarily approaches him from the outside. The writer is primarily the expression of collective consciousness. Free will and the private vision of the artist are taboo. Communism denies the distinction between public and private art. Downgrading the individual, it treats him primarily in terms of the group rather than his own individuality. As everything is politicized, it allows him no autonomous private life. This, in essence, is the issue between socialist and critical realism.

Solzhenitsyn and His Critics

Neo-Stalinists charge Solzhenitsyn with Tolstoyan passivity and pessimism. The critic, V. Chalmayev, in an article entitled, "Saints and Devils," found two moral and ideological poles in Solzhenitsyn's writing[7]: on the one hand, "humility, meekness, and righteousness," and on the other, "all-powerful evil, overbearing cruelty, and blind obedience." *One Day in the Life of Ivan Denisovich* exemplifies the first, Solzhenitsyn's short story, "Matryona's House," the second. Nineteenth-century realism struggled impotently against the forces of evil and envisaged the elevation of man through suffering. Its absolutistic conception of good and evil is incompatible with Marxism. Solzhenitsyn's critics urge that he should become optimistically and heroically active. But he will not surrender his gifts uncritically to the status quo. Solzhenitsyn wills to defend his privacy at the same time that he is a public figure. His opponents charge that his pessimism ignores the lofty ideals and civic interests of Communist society. He believes that they are "whitewashing" tyranny.

The work of the secret police first began to be evident when Solzhenitsyn's friends proposed his name for a Lenin Prize in 1964. They were outmaneuvered by Sergey Pavlov, a right-hand man of the chairman of the KGB. Pavlov charged falsely that Solzhenitsyn had been imprisoned as a common criminal and had never been rehabilitated. He further claimed that Solzhenitsyn had been a prisoner of the Germans. These charges were disproved by Solzhenitsyn's documents. However, they were received too late for him to be a successful candidate for the prize. Previously, there had been attempts to damn him by faint praise: "He is a capable writer, but . . ."

Solzhenitsyn and Fellow Writers

Solzhenitsyn has been very sensitive to the judgments and rights of his fellow authors. Their continuing support was made clear by the discussion of *Cancer Ward* sponsored by the Press Association of the Moscow Branch of the Writers' Union, as late as 1966. Delayed three times, the meeting finally convened in mid-November with fifty-two writers present. Twenty-four spoke out in approval of publication, and none voiced disapproval. Solzhenitsyn's friends compared his depth of characterization to that of Tolstoy and the incisiveness of his satire to Saltykov-Shchedrin, the Russian Swift. Yet Communist officials were not mistaken in refusing to regard him as their protagonist. By this time it had become clear that Solzhenitsyn's views were not faithfully Marxist. Nor was his strategy to conceal it. He wrote:

An individual's life is not always the same as society's. The collective does not always assist the individual. Each person has an abundance of problems which the collective cannot resolve. A person is a psychological and spiritual being before he becomes a member of his society. A writer's duty to the individual is no less than to society.[8]

Solzhenitsyn advocated a society based on an "inner ethic" in criticism of both Communism and capitalism. All strategies must be measured by the moral demands of conscience. His understanding of a writer's mission assuredly has religious dimensions for it deals with "the secrets of the human heart and conscience, the clash between life and death, and the overcoming of inner sorrow." [9]

Today, Solzhenitsyn's works circulate as *samizdat* underground publications in the USSR. Years before his exile, an attempt was made to turn him into a non-person in the Orwellian sense. He succeeded in defying censorship of the most brutal totalitarian type. Soviet control has been more ruthless than any known under the Tsars. Michael Nicholson explains:

> Information regarding censorship and its evasion is as scant for the Soviet period as it is voluminous for the preceding century. The late Arkadii Belinkov drew a distinction between Soviet censorship and that of any previous era: "Before it emerged, dictatorial societies, from antiquity onwards, had been concerned merely to repress heretical opinions, whereas the Soviet Communist Party had introduced a system so thorough that it not only censors a writer but dictates what he shall say." [10]

That thousands of novels and poems remained in the desk drawers of hundreds of authors during the Stalin era is not hard to understand. Solzhenitsyn did not disclose that he was writing until 1961.

To protect it against police interception, Solzhenitsyn memorized at least part of what he had written in the work camp. Of course, the seriousness of literary activity in such circumstances can hardly be overstated. Solzhenitsyn makes clear that poetic imagination could not be suppressed, even in "corrective imprisonment." The rhythm of verse at times clings along with the pick, helping to make life bearable. In a sense, all of Solzhenitsyn's career has been a struggle to publish and control the spread of his ideas in the face of those who would misconstrue them and destroy him.

The Tradition of Great Russian Writers

Solzhenitsyn's characters make frequent appeal to the tradition of great Russian writers. They, too, faced censorship. Solzhenitsyn openly acknowledges his Slavophile outlook in *The First Circle* when Nerzhin, obviously speaking for Solzhenitsyn, is determined not to drown in the puddle of petty compromises. Instead, he will plunge into the sea of experience and live through suffering to the full.[11] The artist should tremble with the utter joy of existence, but he is reduced to subservience of ideology by a series of compromises—all necessary to publish. It is easier to write fantasies than to depict reality. The real threat of repression is that the writer's creative gift will be stifled and lost. Nineteenth-century Russian liberals advocated the Christian values of freedom, equality, and brotherhood, while rejecting their religious base. Solzhenitsyn does not share such optimism about enlightenment, humanism, and national destiny.

Pavol Licko

When the existence of Solzhenitsyn's *Cancer Ward* manuscript became known, it attracted attention in other Communist countries. A Czechoslovakian writer, Pavol Licko, asked to see Solzhenitsyn. Russian officials did not welcome Licko's request. Solzhenitsyn did not wish to see visitors, they reported; he was sick. Persisting, Licko telegraphed Solzhenitsyn and received a reply the same day with an invitation to come and see him. The Russian Writers' Union refused to help in obtaining the necessary papers. However, Licko ingeniously invoked his wartime record and secured help from the Soviet Veterans' organization to meet an ex-soldier. Licko explains what happened:

> First, some officials on the train tried to tell me that the bridges to Ryazan had broken down, that the train

wasn't going there, and that I should leave it in an unknown town an hour and a half out of Moscow. Then I was dumped about ten miles from Ryazan, at a small station in an open plain. It seemed to have no name. After a while, I found a taxi driver and noticed that he had a labor camp number surrounded with a crown of barbed wire tattooed on his wrist. I told him that I'd come to see Solzhenitsyn. He didn't ask the address. He just took me there, refusing to talk on the way, in total silence, and he refused to accept the fare.[12]

Licko has described Solzhenitsyn:

Because he observes the world with an artist's eye and because of his intuition, many social developments reveal themselves to a writer earlier than to others, and from an unconventional aspect. This is what comprises his talent. And from his talent springs his duty. He must inform society of what he has seen, especially about everything that is unhealthy and cause for anxiety. . . . Russian literature has always addressed itself to those who suffer. Sometimes the opinion is offered in our country that one should write about what is coming tomorrow, touching up where necessary. But this is falsification—and justifies lies. This kind of literature is cosmetics.[13]

Publication Outside Russia

Solzhenitsyn was attacked severely for the publication of his works abroad. The journalist, Victor Louis, is said to have carried copies of *Cancer Ward* to the West under secret police instruction. In the spring of 1969, Louis was quoted as explaining:

Legally Solzhenitsyn cannot be charged with anything. Even if, like Tolstoy, he does not agree with the regime, he does not speak out frankly. He uses his dearly bought experience of the law so that no one can criticize him. It is difficult to charge him with having sent his novels abroad, but he is not at all surprised that they found their way there.[14]

Solzhenitsyn was wise and fortunate in the choice of the Swiss attorney, Fritz Heeb, as his agent. The lawyer began legal processes to stop unauthorized publication and to protect Solzhenitsyn's copyright privileges in West Germany and Great Britain. Solzhenitsyn, however, did send *August 1914* abroad and authorize its publication in defiance of Soviet policy.

The Nobel Prize

On Thursday, October 8, 1970, journalists waited outside a particular door of the Swedish Academy as its famous clock struck one. Karl-Rager Gierow, who usually opened the doors punctually at the hour on such occasions, was almost a minute late. Then, wearing dark glasses, he stood before the spotlights and read, "The Swedish Academy has today decided to award the Russian writer Alexander Solzhenitsyn this year's Nobel Prize for Literature."

The citation of the Academy read:

"For the ethical force with which he has pursued the indispensable traditions of Russian literature." [15] Per-Egil Hegge, the Norwegian correspondent, stationed in Moscow, reached one of Solzhenitsyn's closest friends by telephone. The latter conveyed the news to the recipient who did not believe it at first. When Hegge finally contacted him, Solzhenitsyn's thoughts were clear enough. He dictated a carefully composed brief statement and refused any interviews. An *Izvestiya* report stated:

"The Soviet writers have expelled A. Solzhenitsyn from their Union. We know that this decision is actively supported by the entire Soviet public." However, no leading Russian literary figure could be persuaded to sign a protest against Solzhenitsyn's reception of the Nobel Prize.

Possessed of a remarkable sense of strategy, Solzhenitsyn transformed his Nobel award into a cause celebre. At first, he offered to go to Stockholm, knowing that the regime would interfere at least to prevent his return to Russia. Solzhenitsyn is not unaware of the fact that the greater the measures taken against him, the stronger becomes his image as a moral leader. Absent from the Stockholm festival, he proposed to receive the Nobel Prize award in a private ceremony to which leading Soviet intellectuals and dissidents would be invited. The celebration of his Nobel Prize, which never took place in his homeland, was to be a test of freedom of expression in Russia. The fact is Solzhenitsyn is tormented by renewal of conditions which he exposed in his criticism of Stalinism. Political journalism, history, and moral philosophy are all marshaled by him in the hope of preventing the depraved blunders of the past. Solzhenitsyn agrees with Tolstoy's justification for understanding the past. "Look the past in the face and we will understand the violence of the present."

The attack on Solzhenitsyn continued in police harassment. While he was sick in August of 1971, he asked a young scientist friend, Alexander Gorlov, to bring a spare part for his automobile from his cottage in the country. When Gorlov arrived at the small house, he found KGB men making adjustments in their electronic equipment. Solzhenitsyn has described what happened in an open letter to the chairman of the KGB:

> Gorlov stepped inside and demanded the robbers' documents. In the small structure, where three or four people can barely turn around, were about ten men in plain clothes. On the command of the senior officer—"to the woods with him and silence him"—they bound Gorlov, knocked him to the ground, dragged him face down into the woods and beat him viciously. . . . However, Gorlov fought back vigorously and shouted, summoning witnesses. Neighbors . . . came running . . . and barred the robbers' way to the highway, demanding their identification documents. Then one of the robbers presented a red KGB identification card and the neighbors let them pass.[16]

Solzhenitsyn spoke out when the internationally known gerontologist Jaures Medvedev was confined to a mental institution. Solzhenitsyn's letter probably contributed to Medvedev's release.

Without a warrant and without any medical reasons whatsoever, four militiamen and two physicians arrive in the home of a healthy man. The doctors state that he is mad; a militia major shouts: "We are an *Instrument of Power!* Get up!" They twist his arms and take him to the mad house. This can happen to anyone of us tomorrow. It just happened to Jaures Medvedev, geneticist and publicist, a man of subtle, precise and brilliant mind with a warm heart. (I am personally acquainted with his unselfish way of helping unknown, sick and dying people.) . . .

It is time for us to clearly realize that freedom of thought, and locking up people in good health in mad houses equal *murder of the spirit,* a variation of the *gas chamber,* although even more cruel: the agony of the people who are being killed, is more horrible and more prolonged. Like the gas chambers, these crimes will *never* be forgotten, and everybody who has been involved in them, will be condemned for ever, in life as well as after death. Amidst this lawlessness, in which these crimes are committed, it is important to remember the limit beyond which man turns into a cannibal! [17]

CHAPTER IV

Communism
and the Intellectuals—
In *The First Circle* of Hell

Paul Neuberg reports a common joke from the satellite countries of Eastern Europe:

Question: "What is philosophy?"
Answer: "Searching in a dark room for a black bed."
Question: "What is Marxist philosophy?"
Answer: "Searching in a dark room for a black bed which isn't there."
Question: "What is Marxist-Leninist philosophy?"
Answer: "Searching in a dark room for a black bed which isn't there and shouting, I've found it." [1]

Solzhenitsyn would probably agree. In Russia, Marxist-Leninist philosophy is imposed from above by the state. It purports to answer all questions—economic, social, political, and religious. Solzhenitsyn has resisted this imperialism. His early schooling together with his later university career gave him philosophical categories, most of which were censored by the Party line. He has since rejected its point of view and made his own judgments. Solzhenitsyn's style is to offer a point of view about existence. Although he gives no detailed theory of knowledge or doctrine of reality in his writings, he is familiar with the major philosophical systems. Carefully thought out premises surface from time to time in Solzhenitsyn's novels. In the concluding chapter of *The First Circle*, for example, he depicts an arrested prisoner giving up Epicureanism and goes right to the heart of the issue.

Solzhenitsyn and Philosophy

A minimum definition of terms can help to identify Solzhenitsyn's position:

Naturalism (nature only) allows but a single reality. Who is man on such a view? He is an animal, a product of temporal processes. What is the goal of his life? It is pleasure and—most of all—survival in this world.

Humanism (nature and man) distinguishes the human person more drastically from his environment. Characterized by freedom and reason, man seeks to know abiding truth. He has a dignity which sets him off from all other animals and things.

Theism (nature, man, and God) recognizes the physical and human realms and explains them in the purposes of God their creator. The creature's destiny is not simply in this world. His responsibility is not only to himself—or even humanity in general.

Solzhenitsyn As a Theist

As a theist, Solzhenitsyn espouses three distinct realities: nature, man, and God. Man cannot be explained simply from himself, much less nature. He is not the author of his own being or value. Nor is his destiny just thisworldly. Solzhenitsyn's courageous defense of the rights of man is premised on faith in God. He is prepared to cooperate with humanists who, although not Christians, deny the materialistic ethic of survival at any cost.

Communist dialectical materialism is a kind of naturalism. The claim that reality is limited to this level can be found throughout the history of thought. This outlook premises that the organic is secondary to the inorganic. Marx, in distinguishing his position from that of earlier thinkers, labeled it *dialectical materialism*. Evolution, Marx believed, gave his interpretation a more dynamic basis than previous philosophies. For Marx, modern science has shown that the universe is not static, nor is there a transcendent divine Being or beings beyond it. What can be said about the dignity and worth of persons in such a context? In naturalism and materialism the primary value inevitably becomes one of survival, either of the individual, or, as in the case of Marxism, society; God does not exist. The human creature has a destiny simply in this world. Value, thought, and freedom are all reduced to fit within the time-space limits of nature.

Marx borrowed the idea of dialectic from the German philosopher, Hegel. For a period, Marx was a left-wing Hegelian; he continued to use the dialectical method long after he left this school. Hegel's writings are studied in Communist countries today as a background for dialectical materialism. The device is an old one. Plato employed "dialectic" to achieve movement of mind and clarification of concepts through dialogue and discussion.[2] In his *Symposium*, it is exemplified in the ascent of the soul from particular forms to universal truth. Hegel used the term to describe his method. Affirmation and negation, thesis and antithesis, allow for a coming together of opposites in a new synthesis. The end is not contradiction but growth and development. The danger of such usage is that it may become indefinite, a catch-all for realities that do not exist.

> Hegel believed that the "rational" works itself out gradually but inevitably in the "real" course of History, and that this had indeed happened in his own State, which was rational as well as real. This being so, any attempt of revolution or any thought of clandestine activity would be "irrational."[3]

Atheistic Communism

Hegel had held that man without God is incomplete. It is this religious claim which Communism rejected. For the Communist, it is not the divine which makes man; it is man who makes the divine. Myth, cultus, dogma, authority express man's own alienation from himself, nothing more. In religion, the believer projects his needs onto a superior being. Alienation can be overcome when man understands that there is no God. Man must transform his world. It is religion, by rationalizing evils, that prevents man from becoming fully human. Only by returning to himself and the world of nature can man find fulfillment. Religion is in effect make-believe, a record of human wishes and suffering. Desan, a contemporary Christian critic points out the error:

> Marx . . . does not consider the possibility that religion itself might be a natural phenomenon which neither attachment to the world nor dialectic are able to cure. It is possible that the metaphysical structure of man may be one of dependence upon a Supreme Being which is the origin and end of life, and that the act of invocation is not addressed merely to a Myth. From a purely pragmatic point of view, one may wonder whether an atheistic position in which man becomes an all-powerful and self-sufficient center, goes farther toward the elimination of economic alienation. Might not atheism lead to a hardening of relations between men, while the recognition of God could bring with it a recognition of all men as brothers? [4]

Solzhenitsyn's Objections

Can human problems be solved simply by revolution? Solzhenitsyn believes that without moral bases—respect for the dignity of man—revolutionary zeal is impotent. A popular Hungarian pop song runs:

> Tell me, who would you choose?
> Tomorrow, somebody will have to rewrite old myths.
> tell me, who would you choose?
> Tomorrow, somebody will have to redeem the world,
> tell me, who would you choose?
> Tomorrow, somebody will have to tear off his chains,
> tell me, who would you choose? [5]

Solzhenitsyn concluded that Marx's dialectic of history was no more valid than his prophecy that religion would wither away and evil cease. Alienation is primarily personal, psychological, and not just social. No doubt, Marx projected his own psychology on society in revolution. His followers, showing incredible dedication, seized power in Russia and wrought vast changes. Yet there is no evidence that evil has dissolved; in religious terms, man is still sinner. Turner writes:

> Magnifying the problem to the proportions of humanity in general, Marx exempted alienated man in particular from all moral responsibility for striving to change himself. Self-change was to be reached by a revolutionary praxis that would alter *external* circumstances, and the war of the self was to be won through transference of hostilities to the field of relations between man and man. Men were told, in effect, that violence against other men was the only possible means by which they themselves could become new men. Not moral orientation but escape was the burden of this message. Marx created in Marxism a gospel of transcendence of alienation by other means than those which alone can encompass the end, a solution that evades the solution, a pseudo-solution.[6]

But the Evil Remains

Turner argues that the new age which Marx envisaged was really post-historical. The ambiguities and injustice of the present would disappear. No structures would be necessary; the state would wither away. Solzhenitsyn believes that the struggle between good and evil goes on and cannot be understood on materialistic premises. It is psychological, moral, and religious. Revolution does not assure the solution of continuing problems in spite of all claims for a new age. Tyranny follows naive utopian expectation. Solzhenitsyn challenged the accepted idol, arguing that Stalin's terror had its precedent in the acts of Lenin. Ideologically, Lenin was committed to the thesis that there is no justice but class justice, no morality but class morality. That is right which advances the Party. The naively optimistic

scientism of the mid-nineteenth century was accepted dogmatically. All mystery—the fog of religion—as Lenin
called it, could be ended by science.
Neuberg quotes a young mathematician in Eastern
Europe.

You ask me why I go to church. At the university I,
too, was put through the usual courses in Marxism, and I
thought about them, too. And I found Marxism full of
holes. Perhaps religion is as well. But religion doesn't
claim to be science. It doesn't claim to offer a full explanation of everything which, even if it could be given, would
be too difficult for most of us to understand. It just offers
peace in God, and that it gives. And guidance on how to
live, which Marxism doesn't.[7]

Solzhenitsyn would understand.

A Philosophical and Religious Novel

The First Circle is a philosophical and religious novel,
not in the sense of abstract argument but of life concerns.
Solzhenitsyn's characters express a variety of points of
view as they attempt to understand their own experience
and careers. What is existence all about? they ask. What
have been our life goals? What should be those of our
society? These questions are asked in imprisonment, inter-
rupted careers, separation from family, and personal degradation. The characters of *The First Circle* are not just
ordinary citizens, but scientists and intellectuals. Some
have been or are state officials. Solzhenitsyn is able to
describe them because he listened perceptively and with a
remarkable memory during his own imprisonment. In the
end, he does not camouflage his own position. It is not one
of religious triumphalism but of realism. The issues have
been canvased in a contemporary setting.

The first circle of hell is a special confinement institute
located at Mavrino outside of Moscow. It is called a *sharashka* [the word is Russian prison slang]. It is a corrupt

institution with a respectable front. Rather than wasting technical intelligence entirely by manual labor, prisoners —in the work camp language *zeks*—were used in such disciplines as mathematics, physics, and engineering. Persons with special training were confined to this place and worked under Beria and the secret police. The title, *The First Circle*, is taken from Dante and refers to the highest level of hell. Dante did not wish to assign the noble pagans to eternal torment but could not admit them to heaven. Hence, this realm of hell. Solzhenitsyn began writing this novel while he was still in exile, and worked on it for more than three years. Never published in Russia, it circulates today as underground literature.

Life at the Mavrino Institute goes on in a very different way from that in the work camps. Ivan and his fellow slave laborers are demeaned and emotionally starved. The prisoners at Mavrino have food and clothing and are warm. Scientists are bent differently. There is intense pressure to get something done, a compulsion reinforced by terror from Stalin himself. Existing in disillusionment, disgust, and cynicism, the prisoner-scientists live on the lip of the abyss. Any day one can be put on transport to a camp as Solzhenitsyn eventually was. By contrast, those active in the successful solution of a problem were rewarded: liberty, a clean passport, an apartment in Moscow.[8]

Solzhenitsyn recounts that the prisoners of *The First Circle* have a unique vantage point even though imprisoned by the totalitarian state. He compares the Mavrino prison to an ark from which they can survey the whole tortuous, errant flow of history.

The unnaturalness of the situation makes it possible to assemble issues of destiny. The prisoners have time to ponder ultimate questions of good and evil in human life; where else but in prison can one find such time? [9]

It is known that the Dictator is about to begin a new series of purges. In the brief period of time spanned in the story, each prisoner at the institute is required to decide personally whether he will accept the regime's plans and methods.

The principal events of the story of *The First Circle* take place over a period of three days—during the Western Christmas. At 4:05 P.M., Saturday, December 24, the young diplomat, Innokenty Volodin, calls by telephone to warn a doctor who is a family friend not to send the results of his research abroad. Volodin is taken into custody on the night of December 26. His arrest is made possible by the voice identification research done by prisoners of the scientific institute at Mavrino. However, much of the story is not about Volodin.

The scientists have made a huge television set for Stalin and researched a scrambler device which would prevent interception of his telephone conversations. They were also assigned to a voice research project. Human speech was to be broken into its fundamental patterns in such a way that it could be identified for police purposes even when camouflaged by a change in tone.

Unlike *One Day*, *The First Circle* develops a multiplicity of characters. Its narrative encompasses a whole gallery of inmates, guards, and higher officials right up to Stalin himself. The time span of the novel is too short for much development to take place in their lives and thoughts but enough to show who they really are.

Solzhenitsyn's Unique Use of Time
Nikita Struve writes:

Solzhenitsyn has his own experience of time, one which, as far as I know, is unique in literature and which probably grew out of his extended concentration camp experience. Like Dostoevsky, although, as we shall see, in a somewhat different manner, Solzhenitsyn concentrates time to the utmost and maximally limits space. The camp life of *Ivan Denisovich* is described within the duration of one day, *Cancer Ward* lasts several weeks, and *The First Circle*— only four days. *August 1914* is compressed into eleven days. These telescoped time dimensions correspond to an increased density in space.[10]

The dialogue between Nerzhin and Rubin is of central importance in *The First Circle*. Nerzhin's first name, Gleb, recalls St. Gleb, an innocent eleventh-century prince who was martyred by an ambitious brother. Solzhenitsyn describes him physically in terms that are almost a self-portrait; and he seems to use Nerzhin as a vehicle for his own intellectual and spiritual questing.[11] He points out that Nerzhin is a quester who believes that men around him have something to offer. Nerzhin asks Rubin, the old Communist, Pilate's question, "What is truth?" He will not accept Rubin's charge that he is a sceptic or young Montaigne. Nor will he remain within the fraternity of "Rosicrucians," men for whom science and mathematics are an absolute value in themselves. Nerzhin seeks an alternative to the absolutes of Marxism. He believes that man has an organic need to believe in something which is absolute. Skepticism is therefore ultimately insufficient.

Nerzhin is offered continued work at the scientific institute but refuses it. Officials bring in his old university professor in an attempt to convince him to remain. The professor holds out the possibility of a pardon even, in return for competent work. The alternative is a work camp. But Nerzhin angrily rejects the possibility of a pardon, reversing the argument: it is the authorities who need to be pardoned by the prisoners, for the authorities were wrong in the first place.

Solzhenitsyn's portrait of the still-believing old Marxist Rubin is instructive. Rubin sets to work with determination to identify the offender sought by the police. Rubin's background is such that he had not only carried out cruel commands during collectivization but had even informed on his own cousin. Even in prison he still does not doubt Party teaching for he feels that the ultimate Communist aim is so greatly good that it justifies the means used to reach it. Ironically, he rejects the suggestion that the means are wrong—yet his conscience troubles him, and he has sleepless nights.[12]

Portrait of Stalin

Solzhenitsyn was well versed in the gossip of the camps where there were still survivors of the great purges. His portrait of Stalin, although imaginative in its description of detail, agrees generally with other reports. Assuredly, Solzhenitsyn wishes to demythologize the common image of the Dictator and go behind the mask of propaganda. Stalin babbles ludicrously amid his own self-delusions while reading the short biography which eulogized him uncritically. The Dictator's brutality and perversion of decent human values evokes Solzhenitsyn's contempt. And he portrays the consequences of Stalin's apparent loss of a normal human conscience. Stalin is isolated, lonely, unloved; he is the completely alienated individual—believing nothing, wanting nothing, needing nothing.[13] Threatened by informers in a jungle-like situation of every man for himself, lesser officials all the way down to common men were isolated. Community had broken down.

Stalin appears personally in four chapters. Having suffered from his tyranny, Solzhenitsyn depicts him as an aged, decrepit tyrant who dominates a terrorist bureaucracy. A paranoid, megalomaniac, he is surrounded by incompetents. As King Midas's touch turned everything into gold, Stalin turns all to mediocrity. For example. Abakumov, the head of the secret police has had only four years of primary school education. He smashes people's faces during secret police interrogations. Ironically, Stalin is called "The Most Brilliant Strategist of All Times and Peoples," "The Plowman," "Little Father," "Boss," "Butcher," "Great Generalissimo," "The Coryphaeus of the Sciences."

Tearing Off the Mask

Rothberg identifies the classical Potemkin facade which Solzhenitsyn finds in the official deception practiced by

Stalin and his underlings.[14] Illusion has replaced reality. Solzhenitsyn wishes to destroy the facade—to tear off the mask. Solzhenitsyn believes that foreigners have been often deluded by the facade of official misrepresentation. In a section entitled, "Buddha's Smile," he describes an American woman, by implication Mrs. Roosevelt, who comes to the prison on an official visit. In preparation, prisoners are given new clothes, even Bibles. After she leaves, a prisoner who has hid the Sermon on the Mount in his mouth is struck on both cheeks. A similar description of foreigners' misunderstanding comes in a black humor scene. Prisoners on transport are driven through the Moscow streets in closed trucks with the words for meat and bread painted on the sides in four languages, Russian, French, German, and English. A French correspondent, seeing such a truck, thinks it is proof of how efficiently the city is fed. He takes out his notebook and writes in red ink that the provisioning of the capital is excellent.[15]

Direct Comment on Religion

Solzhenitsyn's longest, most direct commentary on religion centers on Colonel Yakonov who is in charge of research at the Mavrino prison. Early in his career, Yakonov was engaged to an ethereal idealistic young woman, Agniya, but did not marry her because of their differences of conviction. Agniya's family shares a long tradition of supporting the persecuted in the past. Now, in the Communist era, she supports the Church. Fame and success will come to you, she tells her fiance, but will you be happy? Two decades later he has reached a position of prestige and power in the MVD. Married to another woman whom he loves and by whom he has had children, he still feels a deep emptiness in his life, a hopelessness, a lack of the desire to live.

Volodin, arrested as a result of Rubin's scientific research, asks what is the most precious thing in the world and decides that it is conscience. Solzhenitsyn is outspoken

against moral relativism. He believes most of all in conscience, along with faith in God.

There is a passage in *The First Circle* where Volodin finds
the diaries of his dead mother and only then comes to
know what she thought and believed. He is shaken by her
emphasis upon compassion and her refusal to participate
in injustice. He is astonished by her trust in the old verities
which seem to him abstractions: Truth, Goodness, Beauty.
One gets the impression here that Solzhenitsyn is reaching
back into his own heritage.[16]

Avowedly religious images also appear in *The First Circle*.
Solzhenitsyn describes the painter, Kondrashev-Ivanov,
who has become a kind of court painter at Mavrino, completing one painting a month for police officials. He received a twenty-five year sentence because he attended a
literary evening where an unrecognized and unpublished
writer read parts of his novel to a dozen friends. Solzhenitsyn describes one of the artist's paintings, a knight questing for the Holy Grail. His painting of "The Castle of the
Holy Grail" depicts a rider on horseback poised on the
edge of a deep gorge. Solzhenitsyn seems to be saying that
what men are really looking for is the city of God. They
waste their lives in a senseless quest for a handful of possessions, never acknowledging their spiritual wealth.

Solzhenitsyn, observing sensitively and as a participant,
knows how much man can suffer. Bobynin, a brilliant scientist, tells the Minister of State Security that once everything has been taken from a person, he is then truly free.
The passage is eloquent, but Solzhenitsyn later adds his
own conclusion that there is always something more that
can be taken from any human being.[17]

Atheism unmasked leads to cynicism; it can only be established in the ethos of the common man by dictatorship.
Solzhenitsyn's view has a wider base, joining past and
present in God's eternity. Time is transcended and yet
given authentic meaning now through a sense of divine
Providence. Solzhenitsyn is convinced that human destiny

is ultimately in God's hand. When men turn away from Him, evil inevitably follows.

Solzhenitsyn's type of realism grows out of his own experience of "border situations" such as guilt, suffering, finitude, and death. Rejecting Marxism, Solzhenitsyn denies that historical process supplies its own meaning. On Solzhenitsyn's view, the battle between good and evil is perennial. He has been to a farther outreach of experience.

The prisoners appeared to their overlords as only barriers to progress, and they were dealt with simply as means rather than as ends in themselves. Why should they suppose that men have intrinsic rights? Marxism gives no basis of its own for ascribing worth to the human person. Solzhenitsyn will not deny abiding truth—as distinct from ideology—or separate time from eternity. For him, Communism has made a radical break with the past and refuses to look at the present openly and without bias. More than it acknowledges, history is a record of grief and pain as well as joy and happiness.

Terrence des Pres points out that the terror tactics of modern totalitarianism have forced a shift to new limits and foundations. There is no longer any rational or affective relation between victim and aggressor. Des Pres insists that the act of survival has value in itself when an individual refuses to die or to give up. Defiance connects "surface experience" with "the thing itself." Solzhenitsyn's life was intensified and purified, and he was forced to encounter the "essence" of reality. Des Pres writes:

> Solzhenitsyn's celebration of life is the outcome of his own apprenticeship. It . . . is something hardly to be known by thought alone. . . . But surely he comes on something, an entrance to the heart of being, the furious purity of an endless energy, of life in itself, something unexpectedly uncovered when the spirit is driven down to its roots, all insolence lost, and through its pain brought to a pristine concentration, and to a sense of finality and quietude that, once again, surpasses understanding. In another age we

might have called it God, God the bleak, the rush, the final
point of a vibrant, unshakable peace.[18]

But Solzhenitsyn does say God!

Nerzhin, the chief character of *The First Circle*, working
as a prisoner at a scientific institution, carries on grudg-
ingly. His real interest is the collection of notes in which
he analyzes the failure of the Revolution. A political prisoner, he wishes to discover how history purifying itself,
came to result in concentration camps. Refusing to submit
to a new work assignment which could win him his release,
he set forth on a "long and arduous journey to Siberia or
the Arctic, to death or to a hard victory over death." This
passage is autobiographical of Solzhenitsyn.

Atheism Is Nonsense

Marxist materialism teaches that a world without God is
more scientific than one which affirms his existence. Solzhenitsyn disavows this claim as nonsense. In the camps,
Solzhenitsyn had to face not only death and suffering, but
the fact of guilt. He knows that the consequences of evil
remain to be lived out by every person individually as well
as by society. His experience has led him to believe that
men will not succeed in overcoming selfishness or suffering
in a new classless society. More often than not, men live in
a world of appearance. Truth is not won simply by abstraction or by retreat into innerliness, but by life involvement. Authentic being is revealed when the individual confronts a border situation such as the threat of death. A key
to Solzhenitsyn's thought is that the dialectic between the
universal and particular is not destroyed as in Marxism but
kept alive in a religious dimension. He is a thinker of
breadth as well as depth.

A sense of radical evil contributed to Solzhenitsyn's
growing sensitivity. It is not a mistake to compare him
with the Hebrew prophets in his experience of the broken-
ness of life. Like them, he refuses to acknowledge the victory of evil any more than the death of God. On absolute,

not just pragmatic or private grounds, he rejects tyranny and the propaganda which goes with it. In every moment, one must refuse the lie else he will be bound by it. Only a man who does so can know real freedom. In this sense, tyranny breeds true freedom for those who refuse to submit to it, but not without the threat of death and great suffering.

CHAPTER V

Dialogue Among the Reformers—
Sakharov and Solzhenitsyn
vs. the Totalitarian State

Ivan Fyodorov was Russia's first printer. A statue of this
pioneer craftsman, cast in bronze, overlooks a small park
in downtown Moscow. Fyodorov stands endlessly scanning
a printed page. Each Sunday, his park becomes a center
for the black market in books. A citizen may pay as much
as two to four hundred dollars for a copy of Solzhenitsyn.
Numerous typewritten manuscripts of *The Gulag Archipelago* have been transcribed from the broadcasts of Radio
Liberty. Some versions are closer to the original text than
others. Often, a customer exchanges only a list of books
with one of the fifty or so chiefs who make the market run;
a group of "slaves" delivers the wares later. But such is not
always the case. The character of the market varies from
time to time, and police surveillance is more severe some
weeks than others. When it is lax, books may pass from
one briefcase to another. The majority of hawkers are not
idealists; they simply supply what is needed to make a
quick ruble. Nor is all of what they sell *samizdat* [the
Russian term for such underground literary traffic]; many
items are books which are hard to secure simply because of
the paper shortage in Russia. Underground literature did
not come into being with the Communists; *samizdat* existed
before the Revolution. However, the reproduction of forbidden books is doubly difficult now since all printing
presses are owned by the state. Needless to say, when

books are purchased in such circumstances, they are read
seriously.

Although Solzhenitsyn's novels are now forbidden reading in his native country, the role of an excommunicate
is not one which he sought. He worked persistently for their
publication. It is estimated that two to five hundred thousand copies of *The First Circle* and *Cancer Ward* circulate
in Russia today. For a brief period his *One Day in the Life
of Ivan Denisovich* provided a window through which Russians could reflect about their own immediate past. Solzhenitsyn made it possible for them to talk about an experience almost everyone had known—imprisonment of some
close friend or relative, if not the citizen himself, in a corrective labor camp. Housing was so crowded that one
hardly dared to speak of this even in the family for fear
of being overheard and reported. Solzhenitsyn, the anti-
Stalinist, became a national figure. However, just as quickly
as he rose, he fell and was assigned the role of a "no-
person"—one which he has resisted. The fact is that Solzhenitsyn has been a successful dissident. All the resources
of the authoritarian state have been marshaled against
him. A lesser person would have collapsed. Irrelevant protest and misstatement could have led to his being crushed.
He chose his cause and audience scrupulously. Most of all,
he practiced absolute integrity. Speaking only the truth,
he called for freedom of information and open communication.

The Struggle for Civil Rights

Solzhenitsyn ranks along with Andrei D. Sakharov, the
so-called "father of the hydrogen bomb," as a leader in
the group of protestors who have worked openly for civil
rights. They have asked only for the freedoms guaranteed
in the Soviet Constitution and in Soviet law, together with
those guaranteed by the United Nations Charter. In spite
of the small number of persons involved, it is important not

to underestimate the impact of their influence. At the same time that the dissidents identify abuses of justice, they seek a podium to make clear the nature of legality and human rights. This is an innovation in Russia! The task is doubly difficult because there is no free press through which to protest arbitrary police action and repression. What is being said in private or in small groups finally makes its way to a larger public. Not only does conviction take on double seriousness and intensity when the individual's career and freedom are staked on it; the outreach of the intellectual as well as the dedicated religious person can be greater simply because there is no open public forum for democratic discussion of ideas and policies. Solzhenitsyn belongs to the creative minority which can determine the future.

The greatest protest has come from scientists and mathematicians, in short from the new technological class. Writers have been the second most evident group. Religious protest, although intense, has not been as vocal. Of course, Solzhenitsyn joins all of these interests in his own person. He knows that *One Day in the Life of Ivan Denisovich* was published because it fitted with Khrushchev's politics. That there was no lasting reform, no change of principle, is evident from Khrushchev's attack on religion. Khrushchev regarded Stalinism as nothing more than a personal abuse of the Soviet system. After the Dictator's excesses had been corrected, Communism was to proceed as before under one-party rule. Solzhenitsyn's protest was more thoroughgoing and one of principle. In fact, Khrushchev did not overcome Stalin's legacy of Byzantine uniformity. Even before Krushchev fell from power, the Party was increasingly in tension with the new technological intelligentsia. No doubt, Communism's power is increased by the Russian possession of hydrogen weapons which scientists like Sakharov have made possible. Nevertheless, it remains centralist and doctrinaire. Innovation comes only from above and by oppression. For Solzhenitsyn, freedom of conscience remains the crucial issue.

Solzhenitsyn believes that a tenacious illusion is nurtured to the present in the West and to a lesser degree in the East: Communism is only a temporary phenomenon and will soon dissolve. A long sequence of broken hopes, destroyed careers, imprisonment, exile, and death itself gives the lie to this ill-founded supposition. To be sure, terror tactics are less massive and overt than before. But both revisionism and the theory of convergence with the West are rejected officially in Moscow. For more than a dozen years following the death of Stalin in 1953, no widely-known writer or intellectual was jailed. A change in policy began to appear when Sinyaysky and Daniel were arrested in February 1966, charged with having pseudonymously published libelous works in the West.

At the end of their trial, they were sentenced to seven and five years respectively in strict-regime camps. Both had pled not guilty. The crassly political character of their arrest was evident in the fact that the prosecution had failed to show any subversive intent. The Soviet press attempted to clothe the proceedings with an atmosphere of subversion, conspiracy, and alleged foreign links. The larger intent was to intimidate the intelligentsia. Solzhenitsyn joined in the protest against this oppression.

Andrei D. Sakharov

Solzhenitsyn has proposed his friend and critic, Andrei D. Sakharov, as a candidate for the Nobel Peace Prize. Sakharov, like Solzhenitsyn, suffers reprisals for championing human rights, although he is still allowed to live in Russia. During the Second World War, Sakharov worked with a group of scientists under Professor Tamm at the Lebedev Institute. His outstanding contribution is evident from the fact that he was elected a member of the Soviet Academy of Sciences at the age of thirty-two, in the same year as his teacher. It was his work on the theoretical laws of controlled thermonuclear fission, together with the work of Dr. Tamm, which made possible the Russian hydrogen bomb. Tamm received a Nobel Prize in Physics in 1958. Harrison E. Salisbury explains:

> The first Soviet experiments in hydrogen fusion occurred months before those of the United States. Sakharov was responsible for this.
>
> It is important to measure the magnitude of what Sakharov did in order to understand the position which this remarkable man now holds in the Soviet Union. He is, in a sense, a kind of Oppenheimer, Teller, and Hans Bethe all rolled into one. He speaks with a voice at least equal to the sum of all three and, perhaps, even more powerfully, since his achievement was greater and more critical. In 1945 the Soviet Union lay at the mercy of the American A-bomb. Less than a decade later she had matched the United States in nuclear weaponry and produced the first H-bomb ahead of her rival for world power. The debt of the Kremlin to Soviet physics and specifically, to Sakharov is immeasurable.[1]

Sakharov, like the scientists in the West, realized the threat which scientific discovery posed to the future of mankind—both in the genetic harm which can be done by continued testing, and the possibility of mass destruction in intercontinental warfare. Even while Khrushchev was still in power, he contacted the Premier, requesting that tests be delayed. Khrushchev's reply was that scientists like Sakharov were not politically knowledgeable and should tend to their own business. As police control tightened following the fall of Khrushchev, Sakharov took an interest in the renewed suppression of dissidents. Still prestigious, he gained access to their trials and recognized the proceedings as a judicial farce. Sakharov and his friends formed a Committee for Human Rights of which Solzhenitsyn has been a corresponding member.

Solzhenitsyn and Sakharov

The contrast between Solzhenitsyn and Sakharov is interesting and important. Both were born after the Revolution and have known only the Communist era. Solzhenitsyn led troops in the war as an artillery officer; Sakharov worked in research and did not see battle. Whereas Solzhenitsyn's disenchantment with Communism came precipitously as he was taken out of battle and sentenced to forced labor, Sakharov's took place when he attempted to face the problems of the atomic age responsibly.

In 1968, Sakharov's "Progress, Co-Existence, and Intellectual Freedom" circulated in *samizdat*. He is concerned about the threat of nuclear war, hunger, overpopulation, and pollution of the environment as well as with police dictatorship. Two years earlier, Sakharov protested the regime's rehabilitation of Stalin. Subsequently, he lost his position and has only a small pension from the Academy of Sciences. His wife's relatives have been harassed and his son arrested. Completing some of his most brilliant research while still young and politically inexperienced, Sakharov enhanced the power of the Communist state in a unique way. Now, as much as Solzhenitsyn, he fears a world in which the new tools of science, most of all atomic energy, can be turned to man's enslavement. Against this threat, he advocates internationalism, contact with the West, and democracy.

Western commentators have been attracted by the dialogue between Sakharov and Solzhenitsyn. At times, it has been interpreted as a debate. No doubt there are outstanding differences between the two dissidents. Yet their common goals must not be overlooked. Both suffer police repression and persecution. In the face of a vast totalitarian machine, they seem small and helpless. Numerically, their friends and supporters in Russia are not large. If Sakharov and Solzhenitsyn had not been known in the

West, in all probability they would have long since been liquidated. The fact is that what both are saying is needed. Neither lives with illusions, and both may be recorded by history as among the greatest of their time.

What Solzhenitsyn Advocates for Russia

Solzhenitsyn finds three mortal dangers in the present situation—war with China, industrial pollution of the environment, and the moral exhaustion of the Russian people. In his open letter to the leaders of Russia he calls for:

1. The abandonment of Marxism as the official state philosophy.

2. Repudiation of revolutionary movements.

3. The end of support for client states throughout the world.

4. Agrarian reform instead of the collective farm system.

5. Development of the Siberian Northeast, with careful protection of the environment.

6. The guarding of Russian economic resources for the future rather than selling them abroad.

7. As much disarmament as is possible in view of the Chinese threat.

8. Release of political prisoners, restoration of civil rights, and government by law.

9. Renewed emphasis on Orthodoxy and the family following the pre-revolutionary tradition.

10. Retention of some authoritarian aspects of the state when necessary.

Sakharov, commenting in the spring of 1974 accepted points 1–4, 7 and 8. However, he rejects Solzhenitsyn's Siberian vision, nationalism, isolationism, distrust of technology, and willingness to accept some degree of authority.

Sakharov thinks that ideology is not primary but only a facade. He cites as evidence the flexibility with which Party slogans are switched from time to time. Sakharov is convinced that the Russian bureaucracy is actually characterized by ideological indifference. Alleged Marxist convictions are actually something else, namely, the perpetuation of power. Ideology is invoked for its defense and strengthening of the status quo. Actually, it dupes the people, buttressing and legitimatizing the system. It is important to note that Solzhenitsyn has written, "Nothing constructive rests upon it (Marxist ideology); it is a sham, cardboard, theatrical prop—take it away and nothing will collapse, nothing will even wobble." [2]

Solzhenitsyn does not expect renewal or reform from within the Communist system. Nor does he believe Western Enlightenment, specifically, a Western type political system will be the nation's salvation. He expects his country to move from one authoritarian form of government to another. "A man can still live without harm to his soul under such regimes—what makes ours uniquely horrible is that it demands total surrender of the soul. What we need is not political liberation—only liberation of the soul from participation in the lie forced upon us." Democracy does not necessarily bring internal freedom. Solzhenitsyn's essays in *From Under the Ruins* should be read against the background of his Nobel Prize lecture.

The Question of Human Sin

The situation is as if Solzhenitsyn had said to Sakharov, I agree with your protest, but what about human sin? "Only through the repentance of a multitude of people can the air and soil of Russia be cleansed, so that a new and healthy national life can grow up." Solzhenitsyn writes of Sakharov:

> Our hearts beat faster as we realized that someone had broken out from the deep, untroubled, cozy drowse in which Soviet scientists pursue their scientific work. It was a liberating joy to realize that Western atomic scientists are not the only ones who feel pangs of conscience— that a conscience is awakening amongst our own scientists too.

But Sakharov's hopes of convergence are not a well-grounded scientific theory but a moral yearning to save man from the ultimate nuclear sin, to avoid nuclear catastrophe. If we are concerned with solving mankind's moral problems, the prospect of convergence is a somewhat dismal one: if two societies, each afflicted with its own vices, gradually draw together and merge into one, what will they produce? A society doubly immoral through cross-fertilization.[3]

Yet a central issue about human freedom has been raised in their discussions. Is it the result of enlightenment? Do men and governments by simply knowing the good do it? What is the role of self-interest and of wickedness? Both men know that the whole context of revolution is more complex than has been recognized in Marxism. Established power does not abandon its rationalizing claims or defensive position easily, be it Tsarist or Communist. Nor does the kind of empirical and mathematical thinking both have engaged in encompass the full dimension of human experience. Assuredly neither accepts Marxist scientism. In *The First Circle* and *Cancer Ward* Solzhenitsyn explored the problem deeply and concluded that there are religious absolutes which cannot be abandoned. He believes in "a power greater than ourselves which makes for good." He does not propose a return to theocracy or religious intolerance. But, for him, Christianity and its insights are a necessary and living part of the cultural heritage.

The Influence of "Vekhi"

Solzhenitsyn's recent essays make clear that he has been influenced by the *Vekhi* volume, a widely debated series of essays reflecting on the failure of revolution in 1905. He writes:

We read *Vekhi* today with a dual awareness, for the failings we are shown seem to be those not only of an era that is past, but in many respects those of our own times.[4]

It gives his interpretation a background lacking in Sakharov—one that is assuredly religiously and politically knowledgeable. With the authors of the volume, Solzhenitsyn looks to the Russian tradition of spirituality. Political alternatives alone are insufficient against an ideological foe. Much of Stalin's rule was simply the continuation of the absolutism which the authors of *Vekhi* attacked. Bureaucracy, intolerance, even the union of church and state remain. Solzhenitsyn assuredly believes in freedom, but it does not stand alone. What are its positive bases, the ends for which men live? What makes life worthwhile? Not forms of government as much as values and community matter. The *Vekhi* critique was relevant under the old absolutism of the monarchy; it is in part relevant under the new Marxist absolutism. It explains much of what has happened in Communism—the spiritual vacuum on which it thrives.

Chapter two of *August 1914* recounts Sanya Lazhenitsyn's reading of the *Vekhi* volume:

> For a long time he still felt that he was backward, underdeveloped, that he could not think things through, to their very core. He got mixed up in a multitude of truths, he was tormented by the convincingness of each of them. So long as he was holding but a few books in his hands Isaakii felt to be on firm ground. When he was a junior in high school, he regarded himself as a Tolstoyan. But then he was given Lavrov and Mikhailovskii to read—they seemed to be right, very true. He was given Piekhanov—true again, and everything fitted in so neatly, so smoothly, Kropotkin—also true, goes to the very heart. But when he opened *Vekhi,* he trembled: everything went counter to what he had been reading previously, but how true! piercingly true!

Gleb Struve explains:

> Whether this little detail is biographically accurate, whether Solzhenitsyn's father was one of the many enthusiastic readers of *Vekhi,* we do not know. But that Solzhen-

itsyn himself is familiar with the book, and that *he* may
have "trembled" reading it, is more than likely. We do not
know *when* he read it, but he could have read it only as
"forbidden fruit": to this day its very title, as well as the
name of most of its contributors (of whom five died as
political emigres after the October Revolution), are more
or less terms of opprobrium in the Soviet Union. Most
Soviet mentions of *Vekhi* are accompanied by references to
Lenin's vituperative attacks on the volume.[5]

The seven different authors who collaborated on the
book did not see each other's essays until they had been
finished.[6] However, their conclusions were similar. Gershenzon, who had conceived of the volume, was the only
one among them who had not been a Marxist. Struve,
Bulgakov, and Kistiakovskii were later associated with the
Kadet Party. Lenin's charge was that the document remained a Kadet one in spite of all denials. Struve, the
most politically active, had shared in the creation of the
Russian Social Democratic Party in 1898 and then passed
over to the Kadets. Together the authors were reacting to
the suppression and executions which followed the unsuccessful revolution of 1905. But they did not put the blame
simply on Tsarist absolutism. Their seven sharply worded
articles attacked the world that the intelligentsia had created for itself since the Enlightenment and called for a
new understanding of justice as well as personal existence.
Cut off from the masses, the intellectuals had become politically irrelevant and impotent. Their alleged moral idealism and call for political change was empty, the *Vekhi*
authors concluded. They appealed to the longer traditions
of Russian history, invoking Dostoevsky, Soloviev, and
Tolstoy, all of whom believed in God. The failure of the
revolution of 1905 made clear the need for change or else
there would be even greater tragedy ahead.

The authors of the *Vekhi* volume were outspoken in their
critique of Marxism. At the end of the year of publication,
Lenin reacted polemically, writing on December 13, 1909,

"*Vekhi* is a veritable torrent of mud poured on the head of democracy." Lumping all his opposition, liberal and conservative, together he attacked it as reactionary. The crisis of the time was such that *Vekhi* evoked a singular response going through multiple editions within a year of its publication. All shades of opinion, left and right, reacted. Bulgakov, whose view of Communism Solzhenitsyn cites in his letter to the leaders of Russia, commented:

> The revolution exposed, underscored and intensified those spiritual features of the intelligentsia which only a few people (and especially Dostoevskii) had previously divined in all their real significance. The revolution was like a spiritual mirror for the whole of Russia, and for her intelligentsia in particular. To be silent about those traits now would not be just impermissible, but positively criminal.[7]

Struve argued that it was the intelligentsia in particular that had failed to give leadership.

> The intelligentsia found in the masses only inchoate instincts that spoke to remote voices, merging into a vague rumbling sound. Instead of taking up systematic educational work to transform this rumble into conscious articulate sounds of the national identity, the intelligentsia just tacked its short, bookish formulas onto it. When the rumble subsided, the formulas were left hanging in mid air. . . .[8]

The Alienated Intellectuals

Most Russian intellectuals were estranged from religion before the Revolution. Berdiaev has described them as a unique group from a variety of backgrounds, not a single class. Those who had had religious training found it of little relevance. Russia lacked any middle class comparable with the one on which Protestantism had built in Western Europe. The intellectuals like the nobility were separated from the ordinary people of the land. The nihilism and rationalism which had emerged in Western Europe in the nineteenth century took an even more drastic form in the East. Many of the intellectuals, lacking any positive program, supported violence. The Revolution came just at the time that some were rediscovering the spiritual resources of the Russian past. It is paradoxical, indeed tragic, that a renewed religious interest appeared among them just before the Revolution, only to be swept away by Marxism.

Kistiakovaskii's chapter continued to have relevance in the Communist era. He charged that the "greatest lacuna" in the public consciousness is that it never advanced the ideal of the legal person. Kistiakovaskii's claim was that the absolute value of the individual and the inviolability of his acts had not been recognized. "It might be said that our intelligentsia's legal consciousness is at the police-state level." The use of detailed regulations by means of written laws in itself bespeaks an underdeveloped sense of law. Today, this can be said of the commissars as much as the Tsars. Kistiakovaskii addresses the problem of Marxism directly. At the Second Regular Congress of the Social Democratic Workers' Party held in Brussels in 1908, Lenin insisted on a siege mentality, winning by only two votes. G. V. Plenkhanov was challenged, "Wouldn't Comrade Plenkhanov deprive the bourgeoisie of freedom of speech and inviolability of person as well."

Kistiakovaskii reports of the Congress:

> But Lenin, the majority leader who insisted on adopting the statutes with the state of siege, was in no way embarrassed. . . . "I am not at all frightened," he said, "by the terrible words 'state of siege,' 'exceptional laws' against particular individuals and groups, etc. . . . It is against fuzziness that we need special, even exceptional laws, and the step taken by this congress has correctly charted our political course by creating a solid basis for such laws and measures." [9]

Kistiakovaskii adds, "But if a party of educated republicans cannot do without a state of siege and exceptional laws, it is understandable why Russia is still administered with the aid of 'extraordinary protection' and martial law."

Mikhail Gershenzon explained, "Our intelligentsia correctly traces its descent from the Petrine reforms. . . . Today's Russian *intelligent* is the direct descendant and heir of the self-owning Voltairean. And the fruit became seed and yielded fruit an hundredfold." In short, what was taken with the Enlightenment and practiced by the intellectuals was the ideas of Voltaire. The skeptical and even nihilistic notions which are balanced off by affirmation in Western Europe had become dominant in Russia. Bulgakov writes:

> Russian atheism is by no means a conscious rejection, the fruit of a complex, agonizing and prolonged effort of the mind, the heart, and the will, the result of personal experience. No, most often it is taken on faith and preserves the characteristics of a naive religious faith. . . . This faith rests on a series of uncritical, unverified, and of course, in their dogmatic form, incorrect assertions: that science is competent to provide final answers even to religious questions, and moreover, that these answers are negative.[10]

Lenin replied:

> "The stormy oratory of the atheistic Left bloc"—this is what impressed itself most on the memory of the Cadet Bulgakov in the Second Duma and particularly aroused his indignation. *Vekhi* simply teems with catchwords like "idolisation of the people." This is not surprising, for the liberal bourgeoisie, which has become frightened of the people. The retreat cannot be covered by an extra loud roll of the drums.[11]

S. L. Frank spoke out candidly against the Marxism he had renounced:

> Contemporary social optimism, like that of Rousseau, is convinced that all the misfortunes and imperfections

of human life stem from the errors or malice of specific
individuals or classes. Essentially the natural conditions
for human happiness are always at hand; it is only necessary to do away with the injustice of the oppressors or
the incomprehensible stupidity of the oppressed majority
to inaugurate the reign of the earthly paradise. The problem of human happiness, from this point of view, is a
problem of the external organization of society; . . . One
need only remove these goods from the minority that un-
justly possesses them, and deprive it of the possibility of
possessing them once and for all, for human prosperity to
be assured. Such is the uncomplicated but powerful train
of thought that unites nihilistic moralism with the *religion of socialism*.[12]

On the other hand, in a passage in *The Gulag Archipelago*, Solzhenitsyn does take note of the ambiguity of
good and evil.[13]

Nicolas Berdiaev's *Philosophical Verity and Intelligentsia Truth* could be taken as an answer to Lenin, who later,
after he had come to power, allowed the philosopher to go
into exile in the West.[14] Berdiaev protested that it has
been made into an instrument of oppression. Thinkers had
succumbed to the temptation of the Grand Inquisitor;
truth has been renounced in the name of human happiness.
Falsely directed love of man—the Marxist love of the proletariat—has destroyed love of beauty and truth, indeed
any absolute value including love of God. The Universal
consciousness respecting the dignity of man and allowing
for the growth of culture has disintegrated. Lenin wrote
against *Vekhi:*

> *Vekhi* very naturally thunders incessantly against the
> atheism of the "intelligentsia" and strives with might and
> main to reestablish the religious world outlook in its
> entirety . . . In philosophy, however, the liberal renegades
> decided to tell the whole truth, to reveal *all* their pro-
> gramme (war on materialism and the materialist inter-
> pretation of positivism, restoration of mysticism and the

mystical world outlook), whereas on publicist subjects they prevaricate and hedge and Jesuitize.[15]

What did Solzhenitsyn learn from the *Vekhi*? Why did Sanya Lazhenitsyn tremble? The occasion of the volume has been surpassed in a second revolution, but not the questions it raised. Not only the liberal democrats but the Bolsheviks as well were swallowed up in Stalin's totalitarianism.

The Tyranny of the Party

The warning against idolatry given to Solzhenitsyn by an old Bolshevik is relevant. Idolatry is not just worship of a graven image, but making of anything less than deity ultimate. Because God is, moral demands are made on men which cannot be ignored. This, assuredly, is the Hebrew-Christian view. There is one absolute good, God, and when men serve anything less, giving absolute power to it, evil follows. Stalin was not satisfied to plot murders; he demanded submission and confession of guilt even to imagined misdeeds. Koestler among others has tried to explain how this was possible. Torture was a major contributing factor. More than this, the Party had been trusted as the last authority. There was nowhere else to turn. To be sure, determined men died affirming their integrity and innocence; others did not.

When V. R. Menzhinsky was appointed head of the secret police by Stalin, the Dictator instructed him to interrogate all those who had been expelled from the central committee.[16] Menzhinsky had his origin from the Polish nobility and was an accomplished pianist. Condemned prisoners who had to cross the inner courtyard of the Lubyanka Prison on their way to the execution cellar often heard him playing excerpts from Chopin or Grieg, as he had installed a grand piano behind a screen in his office. Kamenev, a demoted Politburo member warned him: "Do you understand, Comrade Menzhinsky, where these tactics are leading up to? You'll end by shooting the lot of us in your cellar." Instead of replying, Menzhinsky went behind the screen and started playing Solveig's Song from Grieg's *Perr Gynt*. "Stop playing! Stop!" Kamev shouted. Menzhinsky, looking Kamenev straight in the eye replied: "Why did you ever allow him to obtain the immense power he is wielding already? . . . If you continue your struggle against him, you will break up the whole Party just to get the better of this one man. Do you understand? Do you want to dig the grave of our Party dictatorship and allow the *Kulaks* and the Nepmen to take over? I, too, am an old Bolshevik. I belong to Lenin's brigade, and I shall do everything I can to prevent the breakup of the Party."

But is the Party the last word? Has it the right to destroy human freedom in order to erect its own utopia? By comparison, older tyrannies seem mediocre and small. Solzhenitsyn is not prepared to eulogize Western Enlightenment uncritically any more than were the authors of the *Vekhi* volume. Nor has he bracketed belief in God. Instead, he has chosen to fight tyranny and to resist the lie. Unlike the Communist Party, he does not have to be infallibly right. He is judged by a higher righteousness than his own which he trusts for the final triumph of good over evil.

In the end, the question must be asked: What is authentic freedom and its antithesis, the captive mind? Assuredly, liberty is more than the absence of external control, although it does depend significantly on political and economic conditions. The captive mind seeks escape both from truth and the acceptance of other persons in dialogue. Such was Stalin's strategy. More than this, in his paranoia he "manufactured" enemies. He was not only closed to other people but attempted to impose his own outlook and play God in their manipulation. The clear lesson from the era that he dominated is that such a mind can control a whole population. It fails to grasp the creativity in pluralism, either political or religious. Following his death, Stalin's successors in the Politburo have not acknowledged that freedom requires tolerance of dissent. They admit that they were threatened by his rule, but find it difficult to destroy his legacy. Solzhenitsyn believes that genuine and lasting freedom from the captive mind requires moral and religious bases, not just the acceptance of the so-called dialectic of history. The latter masks opportunism and nihilism. The possibility of another "Prague Spring" remains among persons who have grown up under Communism. When its presuppositions are seen through, there can be only cynicism and nihilism or the possibility of the rebirth of faith as in Solzhenitsyn.

CHAPTER VI

The Human Condition—
Stalinism Tried in
Cancer Ward

Solzhenitsyn wrote *Cancer Ward* at a time when the prospects for destalinization seemed good. Following his release into exile, he lived at Kok-Terek (Green Poplars). In his story, Kostoglotov, who often speaks for Solzhenitsyn, lives at Ush-Terek (Three Poplars). The site of the cancer hospital is the same, Tashkent. There is a kind of "Grand Hotel" setting. Events take place over a period of some four months during the winter and spring of 1951.

The characters in *Cancer Ward*, like the prisoners of *The First Circle*, are a random assortment of Soviet citizens. They have been brought together only by one reality— the disease which threatens them all. Most of the patients in the ward will die soon. It is not the circumstances of the patients' deaths which Solzhenitsyn recounts; the details of their last moments are not a part of his story. Rather, he is concerned to explore the victims' moral and spiritual condition as the ultimate questions of existence and destiny come into view.

Tolstoy's *What Do Men Live By?* is brought into the ward. The book's question would not have occurred to most of the victims under ordinary circumstances, but here it has a profound effect. Podduyev, for example, is astonished at finding the ultimate answer in a book.

Solzhenitsyn's characters are introduced to the reader through the eyes of their fellow patients. The cancer ward, like other of Solzhenitsyn's settings, is in its own way a refuge from ideological dominance. Differences between the cancer victims become insignificant in the face of their suffering. Rothberg identifies two primary ethical foci in *Cancer Ward:* freedom and personal sovereignty, evil and disease.[1] The Party member escapes his fate no more than the exile. It is evident enough that biological and social cancer are juxtaposed in the person of Rusanov; he was one of the most discussed characters in the debate about the publication of Solzhenitsyn's manuscript. At first, he denies that he has the disease, although the flesh stands out in his throat to the size of a clenched fist.

Social Cancer in the Soviet Union

Solzhenitsyn uses Rusanov to exemplify the snobbery, status consciousness, and arbitrariness of the Stalinist bureaucracy. Rusanov's goals are power, possessions, and privileges. His KGB career began with the denunciation of his neighbor, Rodichev. When he checks into the hospital, his wife attempts to bribe the staff into giving him special privileges. He refuses treatment until he is told that he must accept it or leave for Moscow as he has threatened to do. He complies. Asked Tolstoy's question, "What do men live by?" Rusanov replies: ideological principles and the interests of society. Solzhenitsyn portrays him as a coward as well as a bully who has isolated himself from people even before his illness. Although he refers to "Man" and to the Party in optimistic generalities, Rusanov has no real contact with persons and events except through newspapers. He avoids contact by travelling only in his car. His office is reached through a dark lobby that gives the visitor a momentary sensation of having entered a prison cell.

Almost instinctively, Rusanov attempts to rationalize his role in the arrest of the victims whose personal life he has destroyed. His reflection is carried on simply in self-justification and without repentance. Solzhenitsyn probes beneath his rigid exterior into the subconscious and suggests that conscience is not completely dead even in his case. Under the influence of injections, Rusanov has a hallucinatory dream and imagines himself crawling through a narrow tunnel.

After multiple adventures Rusanov finds himself in a coal mine. He lies in a mineshaft, in a gallery littered with small pieces of coal. To his surprise, he finds a telephone beside him. Lifting the receiver he hears an order to come to the Supreme Court. Then he asks which Supreme Court, the old or the new. Awake, he is especially alarmed when he hears the news of the fall of Malenkov.

The Communist cannot discuss death with his wife.

The conflict between Rusanov and Kostoglotov is almost immediate. The Communist Party official insists that Kostoglotov's type downgrades and corrupts the country. Kostoglotov's ideals are justice, equality, and freedom. Confronting the cancer ward officials, he argues against their right to decide for others.

Kostoglotov knows that medical men cure and kill with imperfect knowledge, and he wishes to keep his destiny in his own hands. Solzhenitsyn, himself trained as a scientist, could read the medical books and understand what was being done to him in the hospital. Kostoglotov demands to know his diagnosis together with the details of the treatment being employed against his sickness. He is told that his condition is virtually hopeless.

Kostoglotov explains that he does not want to be saved at *any* price! Rusanov challenges Kostoglotov for talking about moral perfection. Kostoglotov answers that a man should not be stopped from thinking.

Rusanov rejects talk about death.[2]

Hero of Socialist Realism

Vadim stands somewhere between Kostoglotov and Rusanov. He is a Communist of a different order than Rusanov. The positive hero of socialist realism, Vadim is, in life, what

Rusanov mistakenly conceives himself to be. Honest and sincere, he is convinced that men live by their creative work. He admires Stalin because he "exalted science, exalted scientists and freed them from petty thoughts of salary or accommodations." Solzhenitsyn portrays him as lacking humanity because he relies on science. Vadim's disease, melanoblastoma, is the most virulent form of cancer. Vadim's response is not one of blind fear as Rusanov, but anger at the shortness of his life. In his few remaining months, he wishes to compensate for his early death by doing something positive for the good of mankind. He had hoped to find a new way of locating ores by following radioactive waters. Colloidal gold would have been helpful in his cure. In the end, the pain in his leg gets worse, and he seems to wilt. Still a young man, he wants to howl like a wild animal.

Solzhenitsyn signifies his characters' inner condition overtly by outer signs. He has Kostoglotov make the point that mental attitudes frequently determine physical conditions.[3]

The Man from the KGB

Podduyev of the KGB suffers from tongue cancer.[4] Never sick before, he had not reflected on life's meaning. At last, the memory of the young prisoners whom he had sent to their execution while a KGB man, haunts him. Although Podduyev seems to have will power, Solzhenitsyn makes clear that he is only putting up a facade; his aggressive, disagreeable behavior bespeaks a blind, cold terror beneath his outer expression. Podduyev finally reads Tolstoy's *What Do Men Live By?* and is confronted by its teaching that human beings are distinguished from animals by their ability to feel affection. He knows too late that he can never have a clear conscience. His life has denied the love of others which alone leads to authentic happiness.

The Old Bolshevik

The old Bolshevik, Aleksai Shulubin, has cancer of the rectum. He will have to have a colostomy bag if he survives his operation. He summarizes his own career autobiographically.[5]

Solzhenitsyn denied that his writing is a political critique of the Soviet Union under Stalin. Discussing his book before the Writers' Union in 1967, he insisted that its subject is first and foremost, "specifically and literally cancer, (a subject) which is avoided in literature, but which those who are stricken with it know only too well from daily experience . . . perhaps soon, someone among those present will be confined to a ward for cancer patients, and then he will understand what kind of a 'symbol' it is." [6] Some commentators continue to think that he overstated his position defensively; the question of what kind of a symbol it is remains open.

The Ultimate Questions

Although death and dying is not a preoccupation of Marxism, it is not uncommon in Russian literature. Muchnic points out that Solzhenitsyn gives it a fully contemporary setting. The ultimate questions that tormented Tolstoy and Dostoevsky are taken for granted by Solzhenitsyn. Like their earlier heroes, the nature of man is tested in his present-day character. Yet in spite of all similarities, Solzhenitsyn turns their presuppositions upside down.

Thompson Bradley points out the hopefulness for the younger generation expressed in Solzhenitsyn's story:

> It has generally gone unnoticed that considerably before the novel's end the dramatic-moral concern gradually moves away from the older generation (Kostoglotov, Shulubin, Dontsova, and Rusanov). This process begins at that point in the first part of the novel when news of the external political changes filters into the ward with the contested issue of Pravda. The central concern shifts

to the younger generation and forces a new conception
and rephrasing of the vital moral question drawn from
Tolstoy, "What do men live by?" [7]

Early in the book, Kostoglotov advises Demka to take the
"Practical" easier course and give up his plan to go to the
university in search of justice and truth. Later, just before
leaving, Kostoglotov sends him a postcard telling him to
get well and keep his ideals. Demka insists on the obliga-
tion of the artist for sincerity and truth. Rejecting the
counsel that he forget about learning and get a safe job as
a radio repairman and technician, he replies that it is the
truth he loves.[8]

Kostoglotov is not in the end a "victorious figure." Yet
he experiences what Solzhenitsyn's characters wish most of
all—release. Thompson Bradley describes him as a defiant
stoic. But his attitudes and interests are not dichotomized
fully between inner and outer. Solzhenitsyn's philosophy
does not conform simply to that of this Greek school. Un-
fortunately, Kostoglotov is only partially cured. Moreover,
the hormone injections which he is receiving to prolong his
life may render him impotent. When this information becomes known to him, he plots with one of his attendants to
withhold the treatment. Life itself is not the only value,
he insists. It should not be prolonged without the possibility
of a minimum degree of happiness and fulfillment. Discharged from the cancer ward, Kostoglotov again walks
the streets of a Russian city. At first, everything seems interesting and beautiful. This soon changes, however, when
he visits a department store and hears a man ask for a shirt
—size fifty, collar size thirty-seven. Suddenly, Kostoglotov is struck by the contrast between the simplicity and
hardship of life in the camps and the materialism of the city
for which the deparment store is a symbol.

Solzhenitsyn's symbolism continues to be explicit as he
depicts Kostoglotov's visit to the local zoo. Two contrast-
ing modes of existence appear before him. A spiral horned
markhor with its slender legs reminds him of Vera, one of

the women who has helped to care for him in the cancer
ward. Next, he sees a squirrel running endlessly in a wheel.
Drawn to the illusion of sham activity by curiosity, it can
only pass on to self-destruction.

Finally, Kostoglotov sees a tiger with whiskers and yel-
low eyes, characteristics which Solzhenitsyn ascribes to
Stalin. In spite of this figure and the evil which has been
portrayed, Solzhenitsyn's book ends on a note of hope.
Boarding a train, Kostoglotov realizes that his poverty is
no barrier to happiness; he understands that it is possible to
have contentment even with few possessions.

Solzhenitsyn Is a Christian Writer

Dean Alexander Schmemann of St. Vladimir's Theological School in the United States, urges that the key to
understanding Solzhenitsyn's ideas is that he is a Christian
writer. After reading an essay by Father Schmemann, Solzhenitsyn agreed. Schmemann is not concerned to prove
that Solzhenitsyn is a believer or unbeliever, that he accepts or rejects Christian dogma, ecclesiastical ritual or the
Church. His case is not that Solzhenitsyn makes "religious
problematics" central. Rather, Schmemann is concerned
with the way Solzhenitsyn views the world.[9] The triune intuition of creation, fall and redemption is the unexpressed
presupposition of Solzhenitsyn's writing. Father Schmemann finds Solzhenitsyn's acceptance of the Christian doctrine of creation to be evident in his perception and acceptance of the original goodness of the world and life.
Solzhenitsyn will not view life and the world as absurd or
meaningless. There is no ontological pessimism much less
Manichean dualism implicit in what he writes. To be sure,
most of his stories are about suffering, ugliness, and evil. As
a Christian, he does not deny that the world truly "lies in
evil," but his faith keeps him from ontological blasphemy.
Father Schmemann urges that Solzhenitsyn views the
"mystery of evil" from the Christian intuition of the fall as
well as creation.[10] This means specifically that there is no

evil in itself. It is not a kind of independently formed "essence." Yet evil is not merely a negation; it is first and always a fall, one which was unnecessary in a world that was created "very good." Schmemann holds that Christianity is distinguished from other religions and philosophies by the fact that it does not attempt to explain and neutralize evil. Solzhenitsyn is in this "realistic" tradition. He does not attempt to reduce it to a cause, reason or deficiency, but confronts his reader with all its horror. Schmemann sees the Mavrino sharashka and the cancer ward as images of the fallen world.[11]

Christ was not crucified by impersonal forces but by men. Evil is real because it is a personal choice. Solzhenitsyn understands that Christians cannot resign themselves to it stoically, even though it is not they who overcome it finally. This is Solzhenitsyn's strategy for survival, physical and spiritual.

Father Schmemann urges that Solzhenitsyn's intuition is also one of redemption. His religious faith is not a humanistic optimism about progress or the triumph of reason. Yet it is beyond despair. Because of God's reality, nothing is inevitably closed, condemned, or damned. Everything remains open.

CHAPTER VII

The Russian Tradition of Christianity—
Solzhenitsyn's Affirmation of
a Millennium of Orthodoxy

The simple, low Russian Orthodox Church of St. Nicholas
is located on Preobrazhenka Street in Northeast Moscow.
A balding, white-bearded priest, Father Dmitri Dudko,
served the parish for fifteen years until mid-May, 1974.
Church attendance doubled, even tripled in the last
three years of his ministry. He had taken courage to speak
out directly against moral and spiritual decline, vigorously
advocating a return to faith. "With the growth of technology," he commented in a sermon, "the spiritual life of man
can be degraded. I see this as a great danger. The best
minds have come to the conclusion that we can destroy ourselves if this continues." On Saturday nights after Christmas, five hundred and even six hundred persons began to
crowd into the small sanctuary for question and answer
sessions. Intellectuals and young people were particularly
attracted to Father Dudko's dialogue. The younger part of
the congregation did not move in and out as so often in
churches, but remained standing for the entire two hour
period.

Aware that his approach might seem to cause a sensation, Father Dudko remarked, "Have priests stopped doing
God's work?" Asked about the present situation in Russia,
he made bold to comment, "Russia is at Calvary, and
Christ is crucified in Russia." But when queried about the
best time for the Church, he replied, "Now, when it is on
the cross." By mid-May, the Patriarch had forbidden the

courageous priest to preach further. The police closed in and brought Father Dudko's ministry to a close. Protesting his removal from his pulpit, parishioners milled about before the sanctuary circulating petitions. Alexander Solzhenitsyn's priest-confessor had been arrested.

How many priests have been similarly deprived of their livings and congregations? At least half of the Russian Orthodox clergy "disappeared into the wall paper" as it is said in the Khrushchev era. Earlier the Russian Orthodox priesthood had been decimated by Stalin's pre-war persecution. It is true that religious celebration is still allowed in a limited number of places of worship. Not all churches have been made into museums. Many young people show renewed interest in religious mystery, in part as protest against the establishment. Repression is less violent than before. Yet today's polity continues a long history of persecution in Russia. Linked with the monarchy, the Russian Orthodox Church invoked the state against other religious groups for nearly a millennium in persecution which continued until the first decade of the twentieth century. Today, freedom of conscience and the separation of church and state exist more in name than in fact in Russia.

The Reversal of Roles

The contrast between the first decades of the twentieth century and the present is self-evident. Until 1917, the Russian people were united in a state church as most other nations of Europe. With the First World War, an era came to an end. The dream of peaceful progress disappeared, and the continuity of civilization was broken. Christendom was attacked directly. Solzhenitsyn speaks of the disintegration of the vision of man which had been determining for European life ever since the Renaissance. In Russia, the uniform pattern which characterized an isolated and self-contained culture was destroyed. There had been state support for Christianity, cultural as well as political, for nearly a millennium. The cooperation which belonged to the older union of throne and altar is no more. To be sure, a so-called Christian monarchy long persisted with intolerance in Russia. The Russian regime was the most reactionary in Europe. Solzhenitsyn protests very strongly against the persecution of the Old Believers, for example. Today, state power is being used against religion instead of in support of it.

For Solzhenitsyn, Dostoevsky's prophecies have been fulfilled since the Revolution. Irrespective of the nuances of church or state politics, Solzhenitsyn will speak the truth. His open letters addressed to the Writers' Union, to Patriarch Pimen, and to the leaders of Russia, are all attacks on ideology and the lie. Let the writer be a writer, he urges, the Church the Church, the state the state. Stop the lies which are not only ineffective but break down communication between persons. He addressed the Writers' Union:

> It is high time to remember that we belong first and foremost to humanity. And that man has distinguished himself from the animal world by THOUGHT and SPEECH. And these, naturally, should be FREE. If they are put in chains, we shall return to the state of animals.
>
> OPENNESS, honest and complete OPENNESS—that is the first condition of health in all societies, including our own. And he who does not want this openness for our country cares nothing for his fatherland and thinks only of his own interest. He who does not wish this openness for his fatherland does not want to purify it of its diseases, but only to drive them inwards, there to fester. (November 12, 1969) [1]

It is too simple to say that there is a parallel between the Moslem Tartar rule of earlier centuries and Communist policies toward religion. Solzhenitsyn suggests this possibility in describing the Orthodox hierarchy's submission to the invader in *The First Circle*.[2] Moslem conquest brought neither social revolution nor secularism, although like Marxism it confined ecclesiastical life to its own sphere. Isolation is a common experience under both. In his open letter to Patriarch Pimen, Solzhenitsyn points out that the limitations imposed on religion in Eastern Europe today have practical consequences: a lack of theological books, professional and educational discrimination, limitation of travel. An underlying nihilism appears among young people in spite of all party propaganda, as there is no creative base for values or any relation to a larger universe. Life takes on a kind of one-dimensionality when religious resources and perspectives are rejected.

In the atmosphere in which Solzhenitsyn has lived, he has known only a Russia that has persecuted religion. Of course, the intensity of the persecution varied from time to time, and he did attend church as a youth. However, education and police power were totally in the hands of atheists. The twenties were less severe than the thirties. Yet, traditional ways of life were passing as the Church and its clergy were extinguished.

Solzhenitsyn has given his reaction to the situation in "A Journey along the Oka." A new secular ethos was everywhere in which men were allowed to think only of this life. Is it really a better one?

The Traditions

Solzhenitsyn has taken his religious orientation from Russian Orthodoxy. Assuredly, he identifies with the older and longer tradition of Russian life which has affirmed religious faith. Christianity has existed in Russia since the ninth century. The roots are in Byzantium rather than the Latin West, Constantinople and not Rome. Solzhenitsyn's loyalty is to a vital faith which is mediated through a tradition. Liturgy and sacraments are important in it as well as hierarchy and community. Of course, Solzhenitsyn recognizes the importance of individual responsibility for witness and faith. Yet he refuses sectarianism. He is concerned for the religious life of the entire nation. Western Protestantism is not really an option any more than the Enlightenment for him. Solzhenitsyn's Church is Catholic but not

Roman Catholic. Its traditions antedate the Christianizing
of Russia itself.

It is recorded that as early as A.D. 860, a Russian fleet
attacked the Christian city of Constantinople, capital of
the Eastern Roman Empire. Taking notice of the annoy-
ance, the leaders of the empire initiated an attempt to con-
vert the barbarians of the North. For a while, only part of
the kingdom was Christian and there was a conflict with
the older paganism. The Russian *Primary Chronicle* describes the way in which Christianity was finally accepted.
Part of the story may be mythical.

The Grand Prince Vladimir is said to have sent envoys to
investigate the great religions of the world: Christianity,
both Eastern and Roman; Islam; and Judaism. He received
each of their reports in his council chamber and finally decided on the type of Christianity represented in Byzantium.
His envoy had described the overwhelming beauty of the
St. Sophia Cathedral in Constantinople: "Heaven is en-
shrined in the Church, and nothing on earth can equal it."
Solzhenitsyn continues to be inspired by the liturgy. Not
alone the Greek tradition of worship and architecture, but
music and literature, together with a whole system of
morality and statecraft, were appropriated in the Chris-
tianization of Russia. The new religion welded the racially
diverse kingdom at Kiev into a common ethos. It spread
not alone by the conversion of princes, but also by their
political command and by the sword. Prince Vladimir was
so enthusiastic about the new religion that he ordered his
subjects to follow him in a mass baptism in the Dnieper
River.

Religion brought culture to the nation and with it the
pattern of Caesaro-papism. The union of church and state
was taken for granted, continuing until 1917. The religion
of the prince was the religion of his subjects. It is important
that less than a century after the acceptance of Christianity, the Russians were separated religiously from the
West in 1054. Of course, the roots of the division lay in the

difference between Rome and Constantinople. There were geographical and linguistic bases of long standing. The break between East and West was made official when the papal legate placed a letter of excommunication on the altar of the great Church of St. Sophia in the Eastern capital. The occasion could have come earlier or later; its circumstances were quite incidental. The papal legate had not been well received by the Patriarch. The Westerner in anger proclaimed the separation of East and West. The hostility between the two parts of the Roman Empire has continued to the present—now in more secular guise. After Constantinople fell to the Moslems in 1453, Moscow was declared a third Rome.

The Moslem threat did not come alone from the South. Even more important for the Russians was the invasion of the "Golden Horde" [the Mongols] from the Eastern steppes. By 1240, Batu, nephew of Genghis Khan, had established his rule over all the land. Kiev in the South and Novograd in the North were finally subjected. For almost two hundred and fifty years, Mongol invaders held political power. In *The First Circle*, Solzhenitsyn makes reference to the subjugation of the Russian Orthodox Church to Tartar rule. Christianity did not disappear. On the contrary, it kept Russian culture alive as Solzhenitsyn believes that it may still do today. Creative Russians retreated to the forest wastes of the North where Moscow was to emerge as the post-Mongol capital.

The monastery of Zagorsk, forty-five miles to the North of Moscow, is still the most important place of pilgrimage in all of Russia. In a church dedicated to St. Sergius, a priest daily reads prayers before the lighted candles on the Saint's tomb. The sight is deeply moving to all but the most hostile. St. Sergius, a singularly loyal Russian, was at the same time a monk. Offered the office of Metropolitan of the Russian Church by the Patriarch of Byzantium, he refused it, never wishing a place in public life. Yet his character was such that he not only inspired new settlements with their monastic communities in the large open areas of the Northeast but encouraged resistance against the Mongols as well. Religion and statesmanship were so joined in his person that he has been called the builder of Russia.

Initially, the conquest had been ruthless and plundering. From their capital, established in the South, the Tartar overlords demanded tribute. Yet they ruled through local Christian princes whom they appointed; they granted the Church its monasteries and establishment. The bishops and monks came to be looked on as the safeguard as well as the inspiration of native Russian culture. In the end, the Tartar empire suffered from economic ills together with military weakness and was defeated. The Russian Church was liberated from the invaders little more than a decade before the discovery of America. A new era had begun for a still medieval land. The occupation had kept Russia backward and absolutistic, not open to the new events which swept Western Europe. Rather than reuniting with the West as the leadership of Constantinople proposed in the decades before the fall of the city, the Russians appointed their own patriarch and developed a fully autocephalous national church in 1589. It is this history, not the discovery of America, the Renaissance, or the Reformation which most fascinates Solzhenitsyn.

The Old Believers

Solzhenitsyn eulogises the Old Believers as the oldest branch of the Russian Church whose example should be followed today. The background of the controversy which separated them from the rest of Orthodoxy helps to explain his concern for tolerance. The chief characters in this drama of the middle of the seventeenth century were Archpriest Avvakum and Patriarch Nikon as well as the ruling Tsar, Alexei Mikhailovich. Nikon, concerned for the sufferings of Orthodox Christians under Turkish rule, proposed to reinstate some of the Greek rituals which the Russian Church had given up earlier. On first view, his proposal seems unimportant. He demanded that the faithful should cross themselves with the first three fingers joined representing the Trinity. The dominant practice had been to use the index finger and thumb, symbolizing the natures of Christ. Avvakum resisted. There was debate as well about the orthography of the name "Jesus." Although a personal friend of the Tsar, Avvakum was removed from office. He and his followers, the Old Believers, were formally excommunicated. Although they were persecuted ruthlessly and their churches burned, they still have members in Russia today. In short, they were not effectively exterminated. Solzhenitsyn admires their tenacity, remarking that they have resisted the Communists more effectively than the larger party of the Orthodox.

Peter the Great

Peter the Great, coming to the throne at the end of the seventeenth century, was not interested in such controversy. An extended trip to Western Europe reinforced his conviction of a need for drastic change. The mark of Peter's reforms was to remain on the Russian Church for the next two centuries. They were political and secular rather than religious. Solzhenitsyn does not react positively to the secular Enlightenment which Peter brought from the West. Indeed, Solzhenitsyn regards it as debilitating for religion. Like so much that Peter undertook, the innovation was violent and imposed. The priestly class, separated from the people and dependent on the throne, evoked the Tsar's contempt. His strategy was to abolish the patriarchate and substitute a Western style council to rule the Church. Although there was no religious revival comparable with the Reformation or the Counter-Reformation in the West, Peter did oppose superstition. Enlightenment came under the sponsorship of absolute monarchy; the ecclesiastical establishment was brought fully under the dominance of the secular ruler. Peter's structuring of society remained until the 1917 revolution. Russia was a land of nobles and serfs

as well as higher and lower clergy. Neither the Reformation
nor the spirit of the French Revolution really reached
Eastward. It was imperial Russia which was the field of
defeat for the authoritarian Enlightenment rationalist,
Napoleon. The piety of the Russian masses as well as the
ruling Tsar contributed to his defeat. Peter's dream of
modernity, enlightenment, and secularity remained unful-
filled. New Tsars came to power pledging freedom and
liberality only to be overwhelmed in the reaction of the
time. A Tartar style church, a counterpart of that of Ivan
the Terrible in Moscow with its oriental style domes, is
also to be found in Leningrad. It was built to commemorate
the assassination of the ruling Tsar by the revolutionaries
of the later nineteenth century. To be sure, the serfs had
been officially liberated in 1861, but they were faced with
new difficulties and oppression in their changed situation.
The Church remained a privileged institution.

Decadent Religion

It must not be forgotten that anti-religious conviction
has historical as well as ideological roots. In Russia, the
Communist attack on the church has taken place since the
Revolution of 1917. The decadence of the establishment as
well as the need for change can hardly be overstated. The
last tragedy of the church before the Revolution came in
the figure of Rasputin. He swayed the last Empress, a
naively religious person, by his psychic powers and was
even influential in the appointment of bishops. A person of
demonic-like qualities, he was finally murdered. Berdiaev
has identified his appeal to the royal family. They were
isolated from the common people whom they yet in a
strange way idealized. They turned to Rasputin as the
embodiment of those ordinary subjects.

Before the First World War, the *charge d'affaires* of the
British Embassy in St. Petersburg reported home as follows:

It is a curious state of things. There is the Emperor, a religious madman almost—without a statesman, or even a council—surrounded by a legion of Grand Dukes—thirty-five of them and not one of them at war this moment, with a few priests and priestly women behind them. No middle class; an aristocracy ruined and absolutely without influence, an underpaid bureaucracy living, of necessity, on corruption. Beneath this, almost a hundred million of people absolutely devoted to their Emperor, absolutely ignorant, kept ignorant for fear of the consequences of knowledge (by an elaborate conspiracy between Church and State), gradually becoming poorer and poorer as they bear all the burden of taxation, drafted into the army in thousands. . . .

This army, devoted, brave, enduring, religious, will do everything which their Tsar tells them, . . . There never was, I am sure, since the world began such a tremendous engine in one man's hand; not in Napoleon's—because his army depended on his success, but the Russian army is faithful to the Tsar, successful or unsuccessful. And the Tsar's two objects are to suppress the heathen and to suppress the Liberal, and he is convinced that the Lord is with him. How long will it last? [3]

One might ask what would have happened to religion in Russia had there been no revolution. Would Christian faith have been more or less vital and relevant? Could Orthodox theology have given the dynamic for culture necessary in the mid-twentieth century? Russian Christians of the pre-war period cannot be said to have lived in the modern world. Their Tsarist loyalty was outdated and its ethos archaic. Yet it does not follow that a materialistic ideology is an improvement. Solzhenitsyn recognizes the impotence of the Orthodox Church under the Tsars—its sanction of oppression and indolence. It came into disrepute along with the old regime—not without reason. Yet it is not without significance that many young people as well as intellectuals are dissatisfied with the present ban on religious education. Of course, no informed Russian can ignore the older culture and intellectualism of his native land. The tragedy is that the separation of church and state did not come throughout long centuries. In Russia today, there is little direct argument between Christians and Communists, but a living out of divergent convictions over a long period of time. The future will depend more on individual conviction and commitment than on church and state strategies. Solzhenitsyn has attacked the Patriarch of Moscow, the head of the Russian Orthodox Church, directly. How can he do so and remain a professing member of this communion? The answer is to be found in the role of the hierarchy under Communism. After an initial period of resistance, it became completely subservient to the state.

The Metropolitan Nikolai

At the time that the churches were again repressed under Khrushchev, Christians were allowed new international contacts. The Russian churchman most influential in arranging the World Council of Churches membership was Metropolitan Nikolai.[4] Having fallen from favor, he died under dubious circumstances within days after the Russians had been accepted in the world body. Nikolai's career tells much about the role of religion under the Communist state as well as the responsibility and limits of church leaders. One of the four bishops still remaining in office at the beginning of the Second World War, his rise was spectacular in the wartime era. All other bishops had been killed, imprisoned, or otherwise put out of authority. How much had Nikolai cooperated with the state in the millennia-old tradition of Caesaro-papism in order to remain in power? Some have charged that he was employed by the secret police and even informed on fellow Christians. It would be impossible to substantiate this accusation fully whatever its truth or falsehood. It is clear that any cleric left in office during Stalin's persecution must have been in some sense subservient to the regime as a collaborator.

Fletcher argues that Nikolai more than Alexi or Sergius, his fellow bishops, was the religious favorite of Russia's wartime Communist rulers. Part of this interpretation is necessarily conjectural, but based on good surmises. When Poland was partitioned with Germany, Nikolai was given the task of integrating the Orthodox Christians into the Russian Communist empire. Assuredly, the arrests, violence, and executions which were part of this process cannot have been unknown to him. How much did he cooperate and assist the state? After hostilities began with the Nazis, Stalin appointed Nikolai to a commission to investigate war crimes in Poland. His religious office served to support the claim of the Communist state that the massacres of the wartime period against the Poles were perpetrated only by the Western invader. After the war, Nikolai was again called on to help gain the allegiance of the Orthodox inhabitants of the new satellite lands of Eastern Europe. A number of Pan-Orthodox conferences were held under Russian sponsorship.

The continuation of concessions to religion after the war is to be explained in part from some of the same reasons as during hostilities. The Orthodox Church had a good bargaining position even though legal restrictions were not lifted. It helped to facilitate Communist control in the occupied countries and later lent support and prestige to Moscow's peace campaign. For example, Nikolai was an eloquent orator and critic of the West. Of course, nothing could be said independently of the state about social justice. By contrast with his political oratory, Nikolai's sermons were characterized by a sense of personal struggle against evil and by otherworldliness. He was removed from office and died mysteriously in 1961; he had lost favor with the state. It is said that he would have had no public funeral had there not been popular demand. Formerly, clerics were deposed under the Tsars. Nikolai's demise assuredly was not without reason and helps to make clear the limits of Russian churchmanship.

A strong set of statements had been issued on the anniversary of Alexi's patriarchate in 1960. Nikolai congratulated Alexi for preserving religion in Russia without making mention of the Communist state. Alexi replied in the same tone. In the same period, a former professor of Old Testament at the Leningrad Theological Academy was excommunicated publicly. The priest had remarried even though this is forbidden by church law. He was denied his priestly office although allowed to retain his teaching position. Subsequently, he renounced Christian faith and turned to Marxism. Assuredly, his criticism represented a protest against the ghetto character of theology in the USSR and emphasized the need for modernization. The Marxist press heaped praise upon him, but the Church excommunicated him. For a brief moment the Church seemed to defy the state; then ruthless persecution began again.

How could a Metropolitan such as Nikolai submit to the Marxist state? The answer is that he believed the choice to be total repression apart from some form of compromise. He was an intense patriot who joined Orthodoxy with love of Mother Russia. He led a double life, speaking in vigor politically and in an otherworldly manner in his sermons. Nikolai believed that Christianity alone can satisfy the deepest longings of man for forgiveness, love, and an absolute as well as life after death. Communist materialism has limited appeal as set against Russia's past and the present needs of men. None the less, it has political power. The question remains as to what cooperation with the state has really won for the Church. Solzhenitsyn would say—Nothing!

Solzhenitsyn's Letter to Pimen

In June 1971, Patriarch Pimen was installed as the new head of the Russian Orthodox Church. During Lent of 1972, Solzhenitsyn addressed an open letter to him. Pimen had enjoined Russian emigres living abroad to bring up their children in the true Orthodox faith. Solzhenitsyn

asks why this word is not given as instruction to the faithful in Russia itself. Solzhenitsyn writes:

Your Holiness!

The substance of this letter is like a tombstone crushing
down upon the head and breast of the yet surviving Russian Orthodox people . . .

I was especially pained by that passage where you spoke
at last about *children*—perhaps for the first time in half a
century from your high office. . . . I heard these words, and
my early childhood arose before me, a childhood of attending many church services, and it was that uniquely fresh
and pure first impression which could not later be obliter-
ated by any of life's hardships, or by any abstract intellec-
tural theories. . . .

One half century of the past has already been lost, it is
too late to rescue the present, but how can the future of
our land be saved? . . . In the final analysis, the true and
utimate fate of our land depends on whether the concept
of *"might makes right"* will once and for all take root in
the conscience of the people or whether the *power of truth*
will come out of eclipse and shine anew. . . .

To this day, Ermogen of Kaluga is still exiled and confined to a monastery, the only fearless archbishop who did
not permit the forces of a late-blooming and frenzied
atheism to close his churches, to burn icons and books, as
had so frequently occurred in the years before 1964 in
other dioceses. . . .

We dare not even ask about the ringing of churchbells
—but why has Russia been deprived of her ancient adorn-
ment, her most beautiful voice? Would that it were only
churches: in our country we cannot even get hold of the
Gospels. Even the Gospels are brought in to us from
abroad, just as our missionaries once used to take them to
the Indigirka. . . .

A Church ruled dictatorially by atheist—this is a spec-
tacle unseen in two thousand years. Given over to the
atheists' control is also the entirety of the operational
management of the Church and the allocation of Church
funds—those coppers dropped into the collection by pious
hands. Five million roubles at a time are contributed with

magnanimous gestures to various extraneous funds, while beggars are chased from the church steps and there is no money to repair a leaking roof in a poor parish. . . .

By what reasoning could one convince oneself that the calculated *destruction*—one directed by atheists—of the body and spirit of the Church is the best method of *preserving it*? Preservation, but for *whom*? Certainly not for Christ. Preserved, but by *what means*? By *lies*? [5]

Solzhenitsyn believes that such churchmanship should come to an end. He does not wish to talk about consequences but the truth of God. Of course, he knows that there are personal risks, but the position of the state has weakened. Now is the time to challenge the atheistic establishment.

CHAPTER VIII

Religious Believers in Russia Today—
Solzhenitsyn and
Continuing Persecution

Leningrad's Museum of the History of Religion and Atheism occupies a strikingly beautiful Western style edifice near the center of the city. The former church with park and fountain, bears its atheistic title in large gold letters under the traditional symbol of the eye of God. The exhibits give the visitor an introduction to the anti-religious campaign which is still going on under Communist auspices. Part of the materials displayed are historical: polytheism, belief in a plurality of gods, is portrayed dramatically. There are models of Egyptian pyramids and Greek temples. A large painting depicts Socrates with his disciples just before he drinks the cup of hemlock. The account of his life and beliefs, given beneath the picture, seems reasonably fair; the theme of persecution rather than atheism is dominant. It also figures large in the attack on the Russian Orthodox Church. Paintings depicting the burning of heretics, some on stakes and others in cages, are larger than life and cover whole walls. Particularly grotesque and literalistic icons depict hell as well as the deity in primitive anthropomorphism.

Not to be overlooked is the anti-Roman Catholic exhibit in the basement of the building. It has a realistic representation of the court of the Inquisition: a torturer heats up an iron over a scull before three hooded clerics. A complete alchemist laboratory is also included to illustrate the conflict between science and religion. A life-size bust of

Sir Isaac Newton is displayed, but without explanation
that he was a believer in God! Near the end of the hall,
a large oil painting depicts an African congregation ex-
cluding its greedy and bloated priests from the church. A
smaller model shows a jazz combo led by priests. The moral
is clear enough—that all attempts to make religion modern are unsuccessful improvisations. The beginnings of religion are illustrated in particularly repulsive terms: can-
nibalism, beating and cutting, human sacrifice. The oriental
statuary displayed is grotesque and does not do justice
to the faiths from which it comes. All pieces seem to have
been selected as proof of the Marxist thesis that religion has
its roots in fear and superstition rather than any sense of
awe and wonder.

The museum is well visited by family groups, men,
women and children. A special section is reserved for school
instruction, and uses slides and other audiovisual aids. In
a country where the government owns all industries as
well as communication media, it is not hard to refuse the
printing of religious books or the construction of churches.
The unavailability of Bibles and the closed churches, now
libraries or museums, are evidence for any visitor to see.

The Anti-Religion Campaign

At the beginning of the First World War, 54,174 Orthodox Churches were reported open in the country.[1] The
number of clergy matched that of the churches: 47,859
priests, 3,246 archpriests, 31 archbishops and 3 metropolitans in 1912. At the beginning of the Second World War
only a few hundred churches were still in use. Thousands
of edifices had been blown up; others were transformed into
warehouses, garages or theatres, if not museums of atheism. The change had been brought about by the greatest
anti-religious campaign in history; numerically, it far ex-
ceeded the persecution of Christianity in the later Roman
Empire. The Communist regime argued that Orthodoxy belonged to the older order of Tsardom and must be de-

stroyed. Stalin embodied this conviction and attempted to make it effective. Marxism is ideologically anti-religious, not just philosophically, but psychologically. Russian communism to the present professes militant atheism. Separation of church and state is not the same as in the West. Secularization of education, destruction of the Church's influence in culture and anti-clericalism were climaxed by the exile and murder of millions of Christians—bishops, priests, intelligentsia and simple believers.

In *The Gulag Archipelago* Solzhenitsyn speaks of the prevalence of believers among those imprisoned and accuses the authorities of even more arrests than they have reported.[2]

Solzhenitsyn has repeated what was known already, giving it a personal context and interpretation. The Communists did not simply argue about religion, but acted against it. For example, as early as 1918, armed marines entered a cloister in Kiev and murdered the Metropolitan. Solzhenitsyn describes how Metropolitan Benjamin of Leningrad was executed with other clergy after a show trial in 1922. Violence was used against Church officials on Lenin's expressed command. After his death, 2,691 priests and 5,409 members of orders were executed or otherwise martyred in 1924 alone as part of a campaign of confiscation of church property.[3] In spite of all these difficulties, church life was not extinguished. Christians, as it is said, could still breathe. Conditions were good compared to the later period when Stalin had complete totalitarian power and used it widely. Persecution of millions of believers cannot be justified on the grounds that the Orthodox Church was a threat to the regime. On June 29, 1927, Metropolitan Sergius together with members of a provisional Holy Synod pledged loyalty to the Communist government, acknowledging its legitimacy. The sincerity of this declaration ought not to be doubted in view of the Metropolitan's later support of the war effort. Its legitimacy and wisdom, to be sure, have been widely debated. A decade after the

Revolution, Church leadership attempted to reach a modus vivendi with the regime. This was without success. The persecution of millions of citizens proceeded apace in successive waves of terror. Stalin had already made up his mind to destroy Christianity.

The Survival of Vital Piety

By the beginning of the Second World War, the Church was for all practical purposes dead on the Dictator's reckoning. Religion had been rooted out, and atheism had become dominant through police terror. Restoration of limited liberty of religion was not an act of benevolence on the part of the Tyrant as Solzhenitsyn emphasizes. The events of the Second World War made clear that Christian faith had not been destroyed in the USSR. Godlessness was not the dominant sentiment. Stalin was pressed by defeat on his own soil. The military situation and its outcome were in doubt. Soldiers were even kept in battle by the secret police on the threat of execution. The Russian Orthodox Church, following Metropolitan Sergius, was strongly loyal. It sincerely proclaimed the kind of patriotism so much needed for victory. After two years of war experience, Stalin came to understand that faith in God was not dead, and he changed his strategy. On September 4, 1943, the Dictator met the three Metropolitans, Sergius of Moscow, Alexi of Leningrad, and Nikolai of Kiev, and called off the godless campaign. Although the Church did not receive legal guarantees, the office of Patriarch which had been unrecognized by the state since the time of Peter the Great was restored. On September 8, a council of eighteen bishops—some brought in from concentration camps —elected Sergius Patriarch, head of the Russian Orthodox Church. Under the new policy, as much as a quarter of the populace had begun to participate openly in church activities by the end of the war. How did this word reach soldiers in battle—such as Solzhenitsyn? We have no record of his experience. More than this, the years of church reconstruction, lasting a decade and a half, were those of Solzhenitsyn's imprisonment and exile. The postwar era, following Stalin's change of policy, became one in which religion had growing popular appeal. The citizen could attend worship and even identify himself as a Christian believer without suffering the overt repression of earlier terror. The story of the rebirth of the Russian Orthodox Church in the fifteen year period, 1943–1958, has yet to be told fully.[4] Only a vital piety which had survived all attacks upon it could have marshaled the resources necessary for rebuilding in the difficult post-war years. Not only clergy but such personnel as choir directors and readers were needed in renewed numbers along with a host of goods, icons, books, liturgical supplies. Sanctuaries had to be reconstructed and refurnished. Priests came from the young people who had grown up under Communist rule, not just the older generation.

Why does Solzhenitsyn advocate outspoken resistance rather than accommodation to the religious policy of the regime? He knows that the state finally took steps against the Church not out of ideological strength, but out of weakness. It could no longer remain merely passive as religion spread again to workers and farmers as well as the intelligentsia. Atheism had lost ground which must be regained. The Church was not to play a part in destalinization; on the contrary, its role was to be downgraded. 1957–1959 were years of transition for religious life in the USSR. Various anti-religious strategies were tried out before the definitive changes of 1960, supported by a change of leadership in the ministry of cults.

Earlier anti-religious propaganda had been of four types: [5]

1. A philosophical method which based atheism on the principles of so-called dialectical materialism.

2. A historical method which defended godlessness from a vulgar materialistic interpretation of the history of

religion, Christianity and the Church. It is asserted that Christ is a myth; the category of the mythical dominates in the attack.

3. Atheism based on natural science with the premise that science and religion are antithetical and irreconcilible. The senselessness of the Biblical account of the creation of the world is emphasized in view of Darwin's discovery.

4. Criticism of the Church as well as non-Christian religions, exaggerating their weaknesses—for example, the fraud and deceit of the clergy.

Before the war the second and fourth emphases had been dominant. Now, it was decided by the Central Committee, to use the third as keystone. The Church need not be attacked directly. However, the unprogressive character of religion as well as its lack of harmony with materialistic science was to be highlighted. It is at this point that Solzhenitsyn's conclusions in *The First Circle* are especially telling and dangerous.

Although anti-religious propaganda was intensified, the new state strategy was not based on argument alone. Nearly three-fourths of the Orthodox Churches were closed, their number reduced from over 20,000 to less than 5,000. Only three of eight seminaries were allowed to continue. Church life was limited more than ever to the sanctuary. Religious education was forbidden; children could be taken away from parents who insisted upon it. No missionary work (religious propaganda) or community activities were allowed to the Church. On the contrary, the state's educational resources were placed on the side of atheism. A letter of the regime, circulated secretly in 1962, demanded that all children be excluded from worship services. State officials even stood before church doors to see that the priest did not begin officiating until this request had been complied with. Reaching to the Baptists, the letter occasioned a schism in their ranks which remains to the present. Officially, the Patriarchate teaches that a man is called to participate in the fate of his people and lead the life of grace whatever the political system. In this way, it enjoins submission to the powers that be. Of course, a new question has arisen. How much is such submission a Christian duty when the atheistic regime wills the destruction of faith and seeks to drive the very idea of God out of the human mind? Communism premises its ethics and polity on godlessness. The outsider can hardly envisage what it means to attempt to remain Christian under an absolutely ruthless government bent on the destruction of one's deepest loyalties.

How much does the Moscow Patriarchate embody the sentiments of the people and clergy? It is charged that its separation from them began in 1927, or at least in 1943. Such a judgment may be too simple. The roots of the present enslavement of Church leadership may be as early as the revolution! Orthodoxy gives priests and bishops a place of authority. Of course, clergymen who oppose the regime's policies obviously do not come to office or are removed. A survey of Orthodox pronouncements in the Christian Peace Conference shows how much the Moscow Patriarchate echoes the state unqualifiedly. Bishops repeat its propaganda with ecclesiastical covering. Solzhenitsyn knows the history of the Living Church Movement which tried to bring about reform apart from the bishops and ended as a tool of the state. The Partiarchate must be tolerated if one is not to withdraw to the underground church, but this does not mean unqualified trust or obedience. It is the faith of the people which has kept religion alive through their own religious experience and needs.

The religious situation has tended to normalize, on the view of Soviet authorities. What does this mean? No doubt, there is continued pressure on believers as well as the institutional church.[6] 1. Worship or procession is forbidden outside of the church. 2. So, too, are any general religious meetings. 3. The clergy cannot convoke an assembly of believers; in particular, they are forbidden to do so for propaganda (missionary) purposes. 4. No Church concerts are allowed. 5. Church communities cannot organize help for their members, 6. or for other churches or cloisters. 7. All religious societies are forbidden. 8. Parental permission is required before rites such as baptism, confirmation and confession can be administered to children. 9. Children cannot assist in religious services. 10. The clergy are denied any right to instruct persons or groups about their duties. Permission is required from the state for them to function in homes or at the cemetery in case of death.

Konstantinow argues that outward observance is reduced but not belief in God.[7] Marxist theorists with their psychological and sociological studies speak defensively of the ebb and flow of religion. In this way, they seek to explain its continuance and even apparent increase in favor during recent years. Of course, just because a church is closed, does not mean that religious conviction dissolves.

Konstantinow urges optimistically that Russian Orthodoxy has become a "Folkschurch" through persecution. Christians are no longer simply loyal subjects of the Tsar! They continue to be excluded from leading places in education and government and are in effect downgraded to second rate citizens. Solzhenitsyn is not alone in his refusal to believe lies. Millions refuse to believe the lie that God does not exist. Nor are they allowed the luxury of believing that science interpreted in the Marxist context will be able to satisfy all their needs. Common estimates are that at least a quarter of the population still adheres to Christianity.

The courage of Christian witness is not to be discounted, as Solzhenitsyn makes clear in a passage in *The Gulag Archipelago* wherein Vera Korneyeva manages to outwit the authorities and, in essence, preach a sermon to the employees in the office where she is to be interrogated.[8]

Metropolitan Filaret of the Russian Emigre Church asked Solzhenitsyn to comment on "how and in what the non-persecuted part of the Russian Orthodox Church could help its persecuted and subjected part." Solzhenitsyn replied in a lengthy letter addressed to the Third Council of the Emigre Church. The letter throws interesting light on his experience as a young man, as well as on his attitude toward institutional religion. It leaves no doubt that Christian commitment is an intrinsic part of his life and thought as a Russian.

> 60–80 years ago the Russian Orthodox Church, having the full support of a powerful government and being in itself all-powerful and rightful, was shunned and mocked precisely by the youth and the intelligentsia. . . . Now, on the contrary, the intelligentsia and youth in the Soviet Union, even when they do not share the faith, behave towards the Church with a deserving respect, for they have transferred upon the reigning communist ideology all their mockery and despising evasiveness.
>
> That which in the 1930's seemed to be a spiritually doomed desert, today is turning green in many places and directions. . . . With the present weakening of the Church in the West—perhaps nowhere on earth can one find such overfilled Christian churches as in the USSR: there is no room to make a genuflexion, it is difficult to make the sign of the cross, and all this by no means weakens the faith. Feeling the shoulders of each other we strengthen ourselves against persecution. The circle of believers is still much wider than the one of those who can or dare to go to churches. In the Ryazan region, which I know better than the other regions, up to 70% of babies are baptized despite all interdictions and persecutions, and in the cemetaries the crosses are more and more supplanting the small Soviet columns with the star and photograph. . . .[9]

In the 1930s, Solzhenitsyn reports, there was a certain authentic secret and catacomb Church. There is no need to look for such a Church today or to express solidarity with it. Churches are open and believers visit them. As for the hierarchy of the Orthodox Church in Russia, it stands completely at the service of the state. But Solzhenitsyn insists, the sins of its bishops are their own and will never spread upon the Church masses. The body of Christ's Church has arisen and stands anew. Does Solzhenitsyn still agree with his open letter to Patriarch Pimen? Yes. The best way to gain full independence from the state would be an open opposition expressed by the present Church hierarchy. This is what he advocated in his earlier letter.

Solzhenitsyn does not protest the theological straight jacket or liturgical restriction imposed on the Orthodox Church. Baptist or other Protestant ideas do not come within his purview. He does not debate religious freedom or pluralism in the Enlightenment sense. Interestingly enough, his concern is for Church unity—unity of the Orthodox. Which danger is the worst, he asks, the sacrifice and calamities of forceful subjugation or inner disintegration because of disagreements? Solzhenitsyn does not advocate simple submission to the Moscow Patriarchate. The Kremlin regime uses the Church for political decoration and for intervention in the affairs of the international Church. But Solzhenitsyn does propose spiritual unity among Orthodox believers. There are so many steps to climb on the way to brotherhood, and we remain stuck on the lowest one in an incomprehensible division, not in faith, not even in ritual, but in some kind of jurisdiction.

Solzhenitsyn's Model for the Church

What is Solzhenitsyn's model for the Church? Assuredly, not a Western one. One of the greatest sins of the Russian Church was the persecution of the Old Believers, he writes. This is a sin for which the Church has never repented. This oldest branch of the Russian Church is an example for today. Its determination and opposition to the communist regime has been much stronger than the rest of the Church. The first step toward unity should be an all-forgiving reunion with that oldest branch. It is important that Solzhenitsyn does not regard the Old Believers as heretics, but the "oldest branch" of the Russian Church. Religious tolerance is made an intrachurch matter. It is not modernity but conviction which is primary. Solzhenitsyn honors the hierarchy to the extent that he believes that liberation must begin with courageous action by the Patriarch. He is most serious in this conviction. The sins of the Church and its leadership must be forgiven and rectified.

Solzhenitsyn writes:

> However, many phenomena, and especially spiritual phenomena, have a deep and unforeseeable course. The Church, which Stalin introduced as a mere chip in the political game, began, not as an organization, but as a spiritual body, to gather a strength which the authorities did not want to permit, and yet could not fully control. . . . That which had succeeded at the time of the first sudden attack (in the 1930's), failed during the second assault: it turned out that the Church masses did not allow to be crushed for a second time. We, the people living in this communist atmosphere, had already become tempered and fully adapted, as you can easily see from many social phenomena occuring in our country. On the contrary, with its increasing love for wealth, established power is growing each year more decrepit.[10]

It is the weakening of the regime which gives the Church's hierarchy a fresh opportunity, Solzhenitsyn believes. His strategy is a specific and contemporary one for the Russian scene: Let the Church be the Church now. Let its clergy be Church clergy. Solzhenitsyn remembers well the pre-war times when church services were forbidden almost everywhere in the country. Not a single church remained open for services in his home town of half a million inhabitants. The revival of the Church's existence has not come at all from the concordat made by the authorities, but was caused by their disastrous position.

> The strength of the religious wave in the country, in particular because of the restoration of the churches in the occupied regions, and the necessity of pleasing the public opinion of the West. In fact, the concessions and promises

of 1943 were a lie. Now after 30 years have passed—and
with the same unsubdued atheistic anger the authorities
oppress and crush the Russian Church, and they tolerate
it only as far—they think it is only as far!—as they need
the Church for political decoration. . . .[11]

Solzhenitsyn does not argue that the hierarchy make a
concession like that of Metropolitan Sergius.

One has to acknowledge that this declaration was not a
salvation for the Church but an obvious capitulation
which made it easy for the authorities to proceed with
their "smooth" and silent destruction of the Church.[12]

Solzhenitsyn calls for courage:

The sorrowful picture of the subjecting and destruction
of the Orthodox Church on the territory of our country
has accompanied all my life from my first childhood's
impression: How armed guards stopped the liturgy, enter
the altar; how people rage around the Easter service,
snatching candles and Easter cakes; how classmates tear
the little cross I was wearing under my clothes; how
people throw the church bells to the ground and dismantle
the churches to get the bricks.[13]

Solzhenitsyn wrote to Patriarch Pimen in his earlier
letter:

Why, on coming to church to christen my son, did I have
to present my passport? For what canonical purposes does
the Moscow Patriarchate require the (civil) registration of
the newly baptized? One can only be amazed at the spiritual strength and deeply ingrained psychological tenacity
of those parents who go through with this denunciatory
registration, only to be later victimized at work or publicly
mocked by fools. But this is as far as their perseverance can
go, since all the ties of the child with the Church usually
end after baptism. Subsequent opportunities for growth in
the faith are completely barred: participation in the church
service is prohibited, sometimes-Communion as well, or
even church attendance itself. We are robbing our children,
we are depriving them of the inimitable, purely angelic

experience of the church service, which in adulthood can never be recaptured, and the loss of which one does not even realize. Extinguished are the right to continue the faith of our fathers, and the right of parents to raise their children in their own beliefs, while you, hierarchs of the Church, have made your peace with this and support it, interpreting it as an authentic example of the *freedom of religion.* You find evidence of religious freedom in the fact that we are forced to turn over our children—defenseless —not into neutral hands, but to a domination by atheistic propaganda of the most primitive and unscrupulous kind, as well as in the fact that adolescents turn away from Christianity—(they should under no circumstances get infected by it)—have been left with no room for moral growth except the narrow gap between the handbook of the political agitator and the Criminal Code. . . .

Your Holiness! Do not entirely disregard my unworthy appeal. It may not be every seven years that even such an appeal as this will reach your ears. Do not let us suppose, do not make us think, that for the bishops of the Russian Church temporal power is higher than the heavenly one, that earthly responsibility is more awesome than accountability before God.

Let us not profess falsely before the people—and all the more so in prayer—that external fetters are stronger than our spirit. It was no easier in the early days of Christianity, which nevertheless prevailed and flourished. It showed us the way: *sacrifice.* He who is deprived of all material strength always achieves victory in *sacrifice.* Such martyrdom, worthy of the first centuries, was accepted by many of our priests and fellow believers within our living memory. But at the time they were thrown to the *lions,* today one can only lose one's well-being.

During these days, as you kneel before the Cross which has been brought out into the center of the church, ask of the Lord: what else could be the purpose of your ministry to a people which has nearly lost the spirit and likeness of Christianity?

Great Lent

The Week of the Veneration of the Cross, 1972 [14]

Is Solzhenitsyn's strategy a realistic one? What is realism? Christian faith has survived in Russia. Like Maximov who is also a Christian and was exiled in the same period as Solzhenitsyn, he believes that it has not and cannot be destroyed. The appeal is not to Western forms but the Russian tradition and soul. The problem is not that of modernity as in the West. Solzhenitsyn affirms that religion is still alive with power. It cannot and will not be put down. Its life and values should be given free reign and recognition in the culture. It is Russian culture's deepest base.

CHAPTER IX

The Comprehensive Indictment—
The Gulag Archipelago

Solzhenitsyn's career and convictions as well as the present situation in Russia—religious and political—are illumined most of all by his many-sided *The Gulag Archipelago*, Solzhenitsyn's dramatic name for Stalin's system of confinement and slave labor camps. His book, unlike Solzhenitsyn's other works, is not a novel but a record of multifarious experience that came to him while he was confined to work camps, during transit and in and out of prison. A whole subculture with its imposed way of life and underground sources of knowledge is laid bare. Four of *The Gulag Archipelago*'s seven parts have now been published. Solzhenitsyn collected the information over a period of years from more than two hundred living witnesses and victims. The language is often bitter and sarcastic.

> The difference of tone between Solzhenitsyn's novels— with their sometime Tolstoyan overtones—and this work, is in the searing indignation, the contemptuous irony, the sustained passion; equally important the author has been careful to convey what one can only call the hoarse, mocking despair of the prison voice, and its sardonic metaphors, the plain, stinking sense of the cell and the Stolypin cars, the dehumanising effect of a police-culture. A phrase which describes Bukharin and others coming before their judges 'drenched in their own urine' could be written only by one who speaks with an ex-prisoner's voice. The American translator notes the linguistic novelty of the book: Millions of Soviet citizens became fully

familiar with a whole new vocabulary through imprisonment, but this vocabulary did not find its way into Russian
literature until Solzhenitsyn put it there—to the bewilder-
ment of the uninitiated.

Literary rhetoric with its tendency to hysteria is bluntly
excised. (Solzhenitsyn thinks Dostoievsky hysterical and
that hysteria becomes a form of literary evasion.) [1]

To be sure, some of the details of Solzhenitsyn's narrative have been challenged. Yet Robert Conquest, himself
an expert on Soviet affairs, finds valuable new information
in the volume. For example,

the full frightfulness of the highly secret Sukhanovka
prison, which (in my first edition) I was only able to
mention from the evidence of a single prisoner personally
known to me. . . . He confirms the summary execution of
those serving prison sentences as the advancing Germans
approached their camps. . . .

Conquest continues:

One of the categories I had noted was 'Suspicion of
Espionage,' saying that this was a crime perhaps unique
in the annals of world justice. Solzhenitsyn (once again)
demonstrates my inadequate incredulity: For in addition
to listing that, he names the even more extravagant
charge of "Connections Leading to Suspicion of Espionage." [2]

Solzhenitsyn condemns the very idea on which the communist revolution was built, namely, "that some people have
the right to repress others. . . . Even now he believes that
only prisoners understand this and that the rest of Soviet
society remains indifferent to evil because of the claims
ideology sucessively makes on its behalf." The Russian
conscience can be awakened only by a full and open knowledge of the past. Conquest writes that "Solzhenitsyn's
book . . . breaks totally with the myth that has corrupted
and deluded so many commentators on the Russian Revolution and the Soviet regime: the myth of a constructive
and humane Lenin." [3] It was Lenin, Solzhenitsyn knows,

who advocated extralegal procedures and legitimatized the secret police. In Russia today the revolution is not studied so much as history is given a mythical status. Solzhenitsyn challenges this view. "Tyranny cannot be overcome by force alone." Solzhenitsyn's pessimism about the future of Russian society has been criticized; he is not as optimistic as Dostoevsky. Good does not come out of the camps. This is the fact; Solzhenitsyn is realistic. "Underlying the boisterous doctrine are opportunism, skin saving bribery, plain theft and bureaucratic force." Solzhenitsyn remarks bitterly about characters who suppose that "in fifty years or a hundred years life will be better . . ." [4] This can come only from an awakened conscience.

Solzhenitsyn derives his title from the concept of a map of the Soviet Union on which the black dots of the prisons form an "archipelago," "GULAG" being an acronym for the official title of the state prison system.[5]

The Policy of Terror

Solzhenitsyn's general description is at the same time an account of personal experience. The victim begins his way to Gulag Archipelago by sudden arrest—a tap on the shoulder or an invitation for conversation with a stranger at a railroad station, a summons at work, at home, or on the street. Most of all at night, when resistance is minimal, a knock comes at the door. The Black Marias of the blue caps roam the streets where processions have marched with banners the day before. Arrest and search confront a still drowsy victim who has not had time to dress or to collect his thoughts. Inevitably there is his confident assurance that he is not guilty. "Who—me?" It must be a mistake.

Solzhenitsyn describes the traffic between the islands of the archipelago from his own history. Just out of view between two buildings at a railroad siding, huddled prisoners sit on the ground. On command, they rise, lock arms. Clutching their meager possessions—if they have none they may be compelled to grasp their ankles—they hobble

along. Short on their heels are the barking police dogs, as
the prisoners move toward the transit prison. Solzhenitsyn insists that transit cells were built into every railroad
station. Converted passenger cars are called Stolypins after the Tsarist minister who began their use. Although
generally overcrowded, the Stolypins are less dangerous
than the endless red cattle cars filled with hundreds of
prisoners. Travel in the cold of winter means scores of
corpses. The cars themselves are ruled over by a whole
hierarchy of thieves; criminals are mixed with political
prisoners and rifle the possessions not already stolen by
the guards. Wives and families in fact provide them with
loot by sending packages. Women have been known to run
along the cars asking if a husband is inside or elsewhere;
generally, the tracks are barred by the guards. Solzhenitsyn describes one determined wife standing on the hillside
as her husband disappears with other prisoners, of course
to her anguish.

Imprisoned alone, his last night in the Soviet Union,
Solzhenitsyn was told that the charges against him could
bring death. Brutality and terror are not new in the
handling of political prisoners. The Communist execution
of political prisoners has its precursor in Tsarist history.
Dostoevsky's novels bore the mark of his experience with
the Tsarist police. He never forgot how he was led to the
place of execution, to be left standing for what seemed
hours, before he was told that his death sentence had been
commuted to exile. Solzhenitsyn totaled up the few thousand death sentences before the revolution. Some were
commuted; others were passed in absentia. They were meager indeed compared with Stalin's sixty-six million victims
on Solzhenitsyn's reckoning.

Under Stalin, there was neither the intent nor facilities
to treat prisoners humanely. Class enemies were to be
destroyed. The slogan in Moscow was, "We are going to
bang our fist on the table so hard that the world will
shake with terror!" Terror tactics, extralegal procedures

existed from the beginning of communist rule in Russia. How could officials care humanely for the millions of kulaks, the moderately prosperous farmers, when Stalin exiled them en masse as he imposed collectivization? Entire families—women and children included—were piled one on top of the other in deep barges. They were carried across the country, often with no shelter at all, and dumped on the wastes of the North. Millions perished in this way during the first of Stalin's purges. The famine created by their displacement lasted at least three years. This was only the beginning of mass destruction. Of course, a blow was struck at peasant piety as well. Later, party workers, army officials, indeed whole nationalities as well as returned prisoners of war were sent off to a similar fate. Solzhenitsyn's report of the way in which millions of soldiers who had foreign contact were sent to the camps is among the most important new information that he has supplied. His collection of facts was motivated by the intensity of his own humanitarian revulsion while still an officer in the Soviet army.

Solzhenitsyn recognizes that Communist Party functionaries along with the host of ordinary citizens want to go on living life as if nothing had happened; they do not wish to be reminded of the Archipelago. His record of mass brutality and oppression is an unwelcomed one. He attacks the arbitrary use of power, rejecting the doctrine of class justice as no justice at all. He denounces the paranoid rule of Stalin—not the greatest statesman of all time but the greatest murderer. To be sure, Lenin had grown to mistrust Stalin before dying, and wished Stalin's replacement as Party Secretary. Yet it was he who had established Cheka, the secret police, and set the precedents for the greater injustice of later times. Rosa Luxemburg had already warned that Lenin's procedures paralleled those of the Jacobins during the French Revolution. It was necessary for Stalin to exile Trotsky before the purges could begin. He had not yet reached the pinnacle of power when he

could take anyone's life simply by picking up the telephone
or signing his name. But the separation of the political and
judicial wings of the government had long since become a
fact before this time, as Solzhenitsyn notes. Any two
party system or separate judiciary had been rejected by
the Communists. It was Lenin who dissolved the Constit-
uent Assembly in which he and his fellow Bolsheviks could
not attain a majority. No sooner had a village been won
from the White Russians in the civil war than executions
began. Justice is whatever perpetuates the Party.

Solzhenitsyn's claim is simple enough: after a short wave
of indignation in the revolution of October 1917, Russia
settled back to a tyranny worse than that of the Tsars.
Arbitrary political arrests, interrogations, exile and death
have continued for over half a century. It is not just religion which suffers, although it is clear enough what has
happened to Christianity: millions of citizens were arrested
and exiled for their faith. Untold multitudes of the best
trained and most courageous members of society were destroyed en masse. Exile was often only a door to living
death, physical exhaustion and expiration. The nation's
leaders destroyed the most industrious, experienced farmers just when the land needed food; leading engineers,
scientists, generals were liquidated until the outbreak of
the Second World War. At least twelve million citizens, perhaps as high as twenty, were held in unproductive labor in
the camps when they might have strengthened the national
economy in freedom. The camps are not yet closed, although their population has been reduced; it is probably
less than two million today. What is the point to it all?
The facts defy rational explanation. For Solzhenitsyn, the
problem of evil is raised in all its terrible reality.

In his youth, Communism had promised Solzhenitsyn
hope with its vision of the future. It was at very least
pseudo-religious.

Stalin began the cult of the new era, when he swore
fealty over the corpse of Lenin. A pageantry which Lenin

would have rejected accompanied his death. Symbol, ritual, celebration and ideology were not enough in themselves. There was also the suppression of heresy and a new Inquisition. It was the secret police who finally forced submission with brute force and terror. Stalin did not stop with the exile of his leading rival, Leon Trotsky. All other rivals, especially the old Bolsheviks, were destroyed in multiple purges to assure his absolute and unchallenged power. Those who were not taken in the first wave had their turn subsequently. Even comrades who confessed abjectly at public show trials were executed without mercy. But Stalin was not satisfied. Millions of lesser men were fed into what Solzhenitsyn describes as the sewer system. Not only the pious, but men of all types, Social Democrats, Monarchists, Mensheviks or White Russians, were sought out for their background. They were destroyed without reason because of their origin or background, in fear of what they might do, or out of sheer chance circumstances. It could be because of nationality or simply because they were needed to fill a quota of those to be exiled or executed. "Send us two hundred and forty bars of soap," the telegram ran, and when the operator who received it understood the meaning, she too was arrested.

Why No Outcry?

Why did no one cry out, Solzhenitsyn asks. Why did potential victims not flee? But where? Solzhenitsyn was arrested while a soldier in East Prussia and stripped of his rank and decorations. His guards did not know the way past the German lines; he led them to safety. In Moscow, he directed them to the prison which was his destination. Why did he not cry out in the subway? To whom, he asks. To two hundred persons and to what avail? Why not to two million, he asks. One woman clung to a lamp post shouting out to the crowd of bystanders when set upon by the secret police. They let her go but arrested her that night. One can hardly expect that Stalin's madness would

result in a humane prison system. There was spying within
the work camps, dominance by a hierarchy of thieves who
looted for themselves as well as the guards. Millions of
alleged enemies of the people froze to death and why
not? Had they not plotted against the established order?
So it was alleged and they were made to confess.

The highest Party officials feared execution after Stalin's
latest discovery of an alleged doctors' plot; Khrushchev
was among them. The new Party Secretary did not know
what to do with the millions of prisoners after he came to
power and in the end denounced Stalin's crimes. As Party
leader for Moscow after one of the worst purges he had
proclaimed against its victims in 1936:

> These assassins aimed at the heart and brain of our
> party. They raised their evil hand against Comrade Stalin.
> Raising their hand against Stalin, they raised it against all
> of us, against the labouring class, against the workers!
> Raising their hand against Comrade Stalin, they raised
> it against the teaching of Marx-Engels-Lenin! Raising
> their hand against Comrade Stalin, they raised it against
> all that is best, all that is human, because Stalin is hope,
> aspiration, the beacon of all advanced and progressive
> humanity. Stalin is our banner! Stalin is our will! Stalin
> is our victory! [6]

Such mass adulation was part of the Stalin cult. Solzhenitsyn reports how one party secretary had been replaced by another during one of the purges in the Moscow
district. Under the leadership of the new functionary, an
ovation had been begun for Stalin in a large assembly.
It continued, five, eight, more than ten minutes. No one
had the courage to break off the applause. Finally, the
head of a paper factory who was on the platform stopped
clapping. At once, all the ovation ceased. The same night
the factory chief was arrested and sentenced to ten years,
of course, on the pretext of a different offense. "Don't ever
be the first to stop applauding," his interrogator reminded
him, after sentence had been passed. Solzhenitsyn con-

cluded that the greatest utopian revolution in history has become a farce and failure. Clearly enough, this allegation is a threat to the tradition of power which dates from the events of October, 1917.

A society which does not allow free access to facts, but instead imposes rigid centralization and control on all communication, necessarily gives such a writer a great opportunity. There simply is not a plurality of sources of information. Nor can printed material be withheld fully with modern copying devices. The importance of religious faith becomes evident from the strategy which Solzhenitsyn advocates: the retaining of one's spirit and conscience.[7]

In these circumstances, life must be lost to be found! The experience led Solzhenitsyn to challenge the whole Communist mythos at its roots: terror tactics, deception, arbitrary destruction of enemies and potential enemies. Yet his stance is not one of self-righteous pride. He reports that he was almost recruited by the secret police before the war.[8]

The reader is given a first-hand view of the transit prisons. Another transit prisoner enters the overcrowded cell and news is exchanged. It may concern not only the careers of inmates but those of others whom they have known elsewhere. For example, there is Professor Timofeyev-Rossovsky, an internationally known biologist who presides over the Scientific and Technical Society of Cell 75. He had a laboratory in Berlin until the end of the war.

Knowing his experimental animals would die, he refused to transfer it forthwith and leave for Moscow when the Russians captured the city. Of course, he returns to Russia, but as a prisoner, and so meets Solzhenitsyn. As soon as he arrives in the overcrowded cell, Solzhenitsyn is asked to make a lecture to the "Society." Recently, he has read the Smyth report, the official record of the first American atomic bomb. His scientific description is corrected from time to time by Professor Timofeyev-Rossovsky. Solzhenitsyn assures his readers that those who fail to take ad-

vantage of the exchange of information in a wide variety
of human contacts cannot really know what is going on.
They are with scientists and churchmen, generals and Party
officials, persons of different nationality from inside and
outside the Soviet Union. A slow grinding routine is carried on between interrogations. Men with careers in different eras have all been pushed together in overfilled prisons.
Food and water are often lacking amid impossible sani-
tary conditions. There is constant movement from prison
to prison and from camp to camp within the Archipelago.

Explaining Stalinism

How shall Stalinism be explained? The historian gropes
for meaning amid the facts which Solzhenitsyn presents
clearly enough, adding example to example, one to another. *One Day in the Life of Ivan Denisovich* is a very
concentrated, carefully constructed and dramatically telling story. But it is only the peak of the iceberg, as it
were. *The Gulag Archipelago* fills in a wider cast of characters, revealing a more inclusive pattern of life—camp war-
dens, thieves, party loyalists, women and children. Although Solzhenitsyn makes recurrent reference to Ivan
Denisovich, more inclusive questions are asked than in the
novel which bears this name. How was it that the whole
system of concentration camps got under way a decade
and a half before Hitler came to power? To be sure, the
Revolution, civil war, Stalin's purges and the war against
the Nazis all produced new victims—but this is not the
complete explanation for the way in which they were
treated!

In spite of all claims for a new era, the Communists
continued and expanded the earlier Tsarist tradition of
terror, concentrating potentially dangerous persons in special camps. There was no moderation of repression; on
the contrary, it was multiplied a thousandfold. A growing
flood of political enemies was sent to live in the subzero
arctic temperatures of the far North, lacking food, clothing

or sanitation. The majority were not peasants like Ivan Denisovich. Intellectuals—artists, scientists, philosophers, politicians, as well as priests—all leaders in the old order were washed up on the shore of the Gulag Archipelago. Separated from friends and family, they were left to die in inhuman conditions. The victims' fate was to waste away in starvation and disease. Hunger was perennial. Epidemics were widespread. Prison functionaries were taken from White Russian officers, still brutal and cynical. To this oppression was added the violence of criminals. Caring no more for Party ideology than for the lives of other men, they pilfered, gambled and ran from place to place; utterly ruthless, there was little defense against them. They tormented decent men.

The Solovetskiye Islands, in the White Sea, were notorious as a concentration camp area in the opening years of the Communist rule; as a place of confinement, it was among the first and most terrible.[9] Solzhenitsyn's description is detailed and he emphasizes the differences between the old and new ethos. Settled more than half a millennium before the Communist Revolution, the main island had a Kremlin fortress in addition to numerous churches. Isolated and cared for by monks, its economy of farming and fishing was a strong one. Politically, it remained free, by and large, of the pattern of war and imprisonment. The Communists silenced the praise of God; the cloister was set to fire in 1923. Culture and civilization were destroyed with the revolution. The Island was first used as a place of confinement, but the attempt to keep survivors alive receded. Eventually, the door of the cemetery was broken open and executions proceeded en masse in the graveyard. Behind the walls where God was once praised in ecstasy and dedication, men wasted away in agony as they waited for their names to be called. For Solzhenitsyn, the camp in the White Sea is a symbol of what has gone on under Communism—the terrible destruction of human life. He does not defend the old order uncritically, knowing that there can be no simple return to the past. But when love of God has been destroyed, there has come only hatred of man.

In the course of Communist rule, plans were developed for the slave laborers to become a productive part of the economy. Stalinism had its rationale: a prisoner who does not work will not eat. Solzhenitsyn emphasizes that starvation and hunger, unknown before in Russia, came with the Communists. Men toiled literally for their share of daily bread, dispersed in minimum rations. As in the case of Ivan Denisovich, the inhabitants of the Gulag Archipelago were organized in brigades. Their physical labor was to be reformatory. Major use of prisoners was made in the building of the White Sea Canal in the early 1930s.[10] This construction was expressedly at Stalin's command; hundreds of thousands of zeks were employed. Officially, it was reported that no one lost his life in its building. Solzhenitsyn brands this a lie. Tens of thousands perished. Tools and materials were in short supply; when there was no steel, men were commanded to use wood. Without cranes, they were to dig themselves; when there were no pumps, they were commanded to use their hands —all in the subzero arctic temperatures. Soon the Gulag empire became diversified, both geographically and in work assignments. Even before the canal, there had been road construction projects. These continued along with railroads and canals. Zeks worked in building construction and industry as well as in mining.

The prisoners included not just men, but women and children. Soon bedraggled by manual labor, women lost their youth earlier than men. Solzhenitsyn reports that they were often ravaged by their captors as well as men prisoners. More than men, they suffered from being deprived of what they wanted and need most, affection and children. Solzhenitsyn finds a record in the youngest child prisoner, six years of age! Children's brigades—the only ones cared for decently were often joined with those of invalids. *The Gulag Archipelago* depicts a group of children plundering bread from invalids without pity as the latter beg for mercy in the deep pit where both are working. Solzhenitsyn devotes a whole chapter to loyalist prisoners who remained ideologically good Communists, still trusting the Party. Politicals of all sorts were more devoted than before the revolution, he observes. Solzhenitsyn's claim that still professing Communists received better treatment than others has been challenged. Apparently sometimes they were favored; yet the Party's hand was also ruthless against them, destroying not just their careers but family.

In his open letter to Soviet Leaders Solzhenitsyn writes:

> To someone brought up on Marxism it seems a terrifying step—suddenly to start living without the familiar ideology. But in point of fact you have no choice, circumstances themselves will force you to do it, and it may already be too late.[11]

In the end, Marxism was demythologized for Solzhenitsyn, slowly but in principle! The question of Truth became primary. Not the truth of the system, but the truth about life. "Ideology" he writes

> —that is what gives evildoing its long-sought justification and gives the evildoer the necessary steadfastness and determination. That is the social theory which helps to make his acts seem good instead of bad in his own and others' eyes. . . .
>
> Thanks to *ideology*, the twentieth century was fated to experience evildoing on a scale calculated in the millions. This cannot be denied, nor passed over, nor suppressed.[12]

CHAPTER X

Hope From Under the Ruins
(Conclusion)— The Past and
The Future in Creative Tension

The Peter-Paul Fortress in Leningrad is today a national shrine. The visitor can see the cells where such writers as Dostoevsky and Gorky were imprisoned during the last century. There are, in fact, portraits of a variety of revolutionaries—many of them writers—eulogized for their struggle for freedom. What the visitor is not told is that writers are still being imprisoned in Russia today. Russian literature has perennially expressed existential and religious dimensions. The basic dilemma which joins the artist with the religious believer can be identified. Party propaganda emphasizes the achievements of the regime, dogmatically asserting that citizens live in the best of all societies. Ever present moral issues are concealed. The artist like the religious man lives from the conviction that all is not self-complete. The tension between the actual and possible is ever present to him. Neither truth nor morality can be reduced to politics.

Why Solzhenitsyn Protested

Solzhenitsyn's protest must be understood in principle. Most of all, it is directed against what Czeslaw Milosz, also an exile, has described as "the captive mind." [1] The captive mind seeks escape both from truth and the acceptance of other persons in dialogue. Such was Stalin's strategy. More than this, in his paranoia he "manufactured" enemies. He was not only closed to other people but at-

122

tempted to impose his own outlook and play God in their manipulation. The clear lesson from the era that he dominated is that such a mind can control a whole population. It fails to grasp the creativity in pluralism, either political or religious. Following his death, Stalin's successors in the politburo have not acknowledged that freedom requires tolerance of dissent. They admit that they were threatened by his rule, but find it difficult to destroy his legacy. Solzhenitsyn believes that genuine and lasting freedom from the captive mind requires moral and religious bases. When totalitarianism is seen through, there can be only cynicism or the possibility of the rebirth of faith.

The following comment circulated in Western Europe following Solzhenitsyn's exile: "Everyone in the West agrees with him! The silencing of dissidents, arbitrary arrests, and abuse of human rights should stop. But what can anyone do? Nothing happens in Eastern Europe!" Solzhenitsyn, of course, does not accept this stance of impotence. However, on second reading, the consensus about him in the West is not as great as it first seemed to be. In the West as much as the East, he is still his own man. He criticizes superficial internationalism and is by contrast a Slavophile of sorts, steeped in the writings of Dostoevsky and Tolstoy. Solzhenitsyn is critical of any naive belief in modernity as reforming human nature; progress is challenged. He regards Western young people as too often nihilistic. In his Nobel Prize address, he even criticized the United Nations as representing governments rather than their people.[2] He is against great cities and seems unmodern in his attitude toward women. He does not champion their rights. Western readers still expect that a writer who has spent all of his lifetime amid censorship and repression will be unfailingly well-informed on every question. They look for agreement in detail more than in principle and are often disappointed.

Of course, Solzhenitsyn recognizes the difference between a totalitarian centralist society and a more plural-

istic one. Faced with Stalinist repression, history became
singularly important for him. This is especially the case
because he regards the last fifty years of Communist rule
as an unnecessary and unwarranted break with the past.
He is deeply Russian, and this is reflected in his faith. His
sentiments are those of a pre-1848 nationalist, not exclu-
sive or chauvinistic, but loyal. Many of the responses in his
literary works are to be explained from this background.
It would be naive to think that civilization or religion begin again in any single lifetime. So to think would be to
remain rootless. Most of all, Solzhenitsyn wishes to return
to Russia. This very fact makes clear that he does not look
to the West for inspiration.

Solzhenitsyn recognizes that the modern claim to have
displaced religion is not found in Marxism alone. The so-
called secular view no longer understands life as a mystery to be lived with but as a problem to be solved. In fact,
a myth is involved, namely, that time alone will overcome
tenacious evils, culture lags, and selfishness.

Solzhenitsyn's critique is directed against a rootless, secular view of man's life. So-called moderns too often view
freedom as simply negative, the absence of restraint. Positive affirmation requires goals, direction, support in reality.
Of course, categorical anti-communism is not enough. Non-
Marxists who flount the truth by their actions are no better
than the ideology they criticize. Solzhenitsyn would not
deny the importance of revisionism as in Czechoslovakia,
but he knows that it has been suppressed. He concludes
that the view of the world dominant since the Renaissance
is threatened by modern nihilism. The spirit of Munich,
one of cowardice and weakness, is still rampant.

> The spirit of Munich has by no means retreated into the
> past, it was no short-lived episode. I would even dare to
> claim that the spirit of Munich dominates the twentieth
> century. A timorous civilized world, faced with the on-
> slaught of a suddenly revived and snarling barbarism, has
> found nothing to oppose it with except concessions and

smiles. The spirit of Munich is a malady of the will of affluent people; it is the chronic state of those who have abandoned themselves to the pursuit of prosperity at any price, who have succumbed to a belief in material well-being as the principal goal of life on earth. Such people—and there are many in today's world—choose passivity and retreat, just so long as their accustomed life can be made to last a little longer, just so long as the transition to hardship can be put off for another day; and tomorrow—who knows?—everything may turn out to be all right . . . (But it never will! The price paid for cowardice will not only be the more exorbitant. Courage and victory come to us only when we are resolved to make sacrifices.) [3]

Detente may make it possible for human life to continue throughout the remainder of this century without hydrogen warfare, but what kind of life!

The Role of Religion

What is the role of religion in such circumstances?

Solzhenitsyn has given his verdict on the world's great religions. In imprisonment, he concluded that the dividing line between good and evil is not between states or parties, but in the human heart. There is good and evil in the same heart. Religions fight the evil that exists in all men.[4] Revolutions destroy the bearers of evil but not evil itself. Solzhenitsyn does not agree with those who see the world simply in terms of black and white, in the West any more than the East. He recounts that he was given a comfortable room and bed—even a bed table—early in his imprisonment. An attempt was made to win him over—into submission. The world is divided into two sides, capitalist and Communist, he was told by his interrogator. You must choose which side you wish to serve. Are you really a Soviet man by intention? Solzhenitsyn was never convinced. The matter is not that simple. His religious reference distinguishes his judgment from other critiques of Communism, giving his interpretation a positive basis. Milosz comments: "It is also possible to argue that faith and lack of faith,

good and evil, remain for men vague notions unless they
have spent a few years in a labor camp." [5] Solzhenitsyn's
entire outlook is inexplicable apart from this experience.

Solzhenitsyn calls attention to the absence of suicide
among the zeks. Prisoners died by hundreds of thousands
and millions in the camps, but not by their own hand. In
fact, there was less self-destruction among them than in the
outside world. To be sure, for non-Russians, imprisonment
was a more catastrophic blow, and the incidence of suicide
was higher.

Unlike prisoners in Dostoevsky's novels, the zeks of *The
Gulag Archipelago* are not conscious of any guilt. A sense
of national afflictions similar to that felt under the Tartar
yoke helps to preserve life.

Will Stalinism Return?

Stalin was the author of the totalitarian centralism
which required the work camps for reinforcement. Solzhenitsyn fears most of all the return of Stalinism in the
growing repression of the present regime. Has he misjudged
the Dictator? Trotsky wrote from his exile:

> Stalin has established a system of atrocious privileges.
> . . . Where and when has the human personality been so
> humiliated as in the U.S.S.R. Socialism would be point-
> less outside a society marked by unselfish, honest, human
> relations between people. Stalin's regime has permeated
> social and personal relations with lies, careerism and be-
> trayal.[6]

Khrushchev wrote in his remembrances of Stalin:

> His pretensions to a very special role in our history are
> well founded, for he really was a man of outstanding skill
> and intelligence. . . . In everything about Stalin's personal-
> ity there was something admirable and correct as well as
> something savage. Nevertheless, if he were alive today, I
> would vote that he should be brought to trial and punished
> for his crimes.[7]

What is the difference between Solzhenitsyn's and these earlier challenges of Trotsky and Khrushchev? His has stronger moral and religious bases. They are not abstract but concrete, and he is willing to fight for them. Stalin's daughter's appraisal of the crimes against which Solzhenitsyn protests is not to be ignored any more than her affirmation of faith in God.

> He [Stalin] gave his name to this bloodbath of absolute dictatorship. He knew what he was doing. He was neither insane nor misled. With cold calculation he had cemented his own power, afraid of losing it more than anything else in the world. And so his first concentrated drive had been the liquidation of his enemies and rivals. The rest followed later.[8]

Stalin as a political prisoner before the First World War was compelled to run the gauntlet while the guards beat the prisoners with their weapons. He is reported to have walked and not run down the line, reading a book by Marx.[9] No doubt, the young agitator read the book in anticipation of the Revolution. Stalin's growing atheism, before he began his career as a revolutionary, has been recounted by a fellow student named Pavkadze. Stalin loaned him a copy of Feuerbach's *Essence of Christianity* from which Marx had taken his critique of religion. "The first thing we had to do, he would say, was to become atheists. Many of us thus began to acquire a materialistic outlook and to ignore theological studies." Another student named Glurdjidze recalled speaking once to Stalin about the living God. "You know, they are fooling us. There is no God," Stalin told him. The story is that he offered to lend his fellow student a volume which would show that talk about God is sheer nonsense. The book was Darwin's *Descent of Man*. Some thirty years later, Stalin told a Finnish correspondent:

> If God exists, he must have ordained slavery, feudalism and capitalism; he must want humanity to suffer, as the

monks were always telling me. Then there would be no
hope for the toiling masses to free themselves from their
oppressors. I knew that humanity could fight its way to
freedom.[10]

Solzhenitsyn's Views of Freedom

By contrast, Solzhenitsyn views freedom differently. His
experience has its background not in Darwin but in the
works of Dostoevsky and Tolstoy, both of whom he knows
very well. Dostoevsky probed the dimension of belief and
unbelief—suffering from his prison experience. However, it
is Tolstoy who raised drastic questions about the establishment. The Orthodox Church was a part of Tsardom; for
Tolstoy, this had little or nothing to do with the religion
of Jesus. Unlike Tolstoy, Solzhenitsyn was a soldier and
still preserves a sense of patriotic duty from his military experience. He is not prepared to retreat into innerliness: the
pressures are too great to allow him to do so. His enemies
charge that he is a reactionary, attempting to identify
him with the old regime. How much does the ethos of
Tsardom linger on in Solzhenitsyn? At this point, a comparison with Tolstoy is important and more creative than
on first appearance.

Solzhenitsyn's *August 1914* is a historical-philosophical
novel. The crisis of the Revolution has remained fundamental in his consciousness. Solzhenitsyn had decided on
this part of his life work—research and writing such a book
—before the Second World War and continues to regard
it as a major focus. There are now reports that he intends
to carry the story past October, 1916, and March, 1917, to
the Revolution itself. A broad gallery of characters appears
in his description of pre-war society. *August 1914* has
sixty-four chapters with fifty-five episodes, two flashbacks,
four summaries, and three montages of newspaper clip-
pings. It is an all-encompassing reconstruction of Russian
life on the eve of a great upheaval. It is also a searching

inquiry into the causes of its disintegration. Solzhenitsyn is looking for historical roots. For him, the defeat of General Samsonov's army in the early days of the First World War was much more than a lost battle; it was rather the turning point when a hole was opened at the bottom of the "lake" of national life, and the water of the lake began to drain away from it forever.

As in *Cancer Ward*, Tolstoy's reflections raise basic moral and religious questions. In fact, Tolstoy's *War and Peace* is in the background of Solzhenitsyn's entire narrative. Solzhenitsyn describes a meeting between Tolstoy and a youth. The Sage's dictum of love as the only law is challenged. The young man volunteers for the army, rejecting Tolstoy's belief in non-resistance. Schmemann finds Tolstoyans in the novel

> in the Imperial Court, firmly convinced that God cannot be other than "with Russia," and that the Mother of God would never allow L'vov to fall. And underneath all this religio-patriotic unction, the "nicest" and "kindest" courtiers and generals; either to please "higher-ups" or by conviction, question the soldiers not about whether they have resisted or eaten, but about the parish feats in their village. And as a result, they are fearfully and senselessly routed, in the tragic inevitability of that rout, they point to the inevitable end. This is the basic theme of *August 1914*; a terribly simple and bitter one.[11]

But Tolstoy rejected violence and criticized the abuse of rank and authority in the army. Here one comes to the central issue. Tolstoy's theory was that no order by any general, including Napoleon himself, can change the course of history. This determinism is joined to the belief that the universals of human thought are by and large unknowable. Toystoy idealized Field Marshal Kutuzov, who in the end won over Napoleon. This Russian knew the ceaseless flow of history. Following his instincts, he surrendered to them and emerged victorious. Napoleon, the

Enlightenment Frenchman, seduced by nationalism, attempted to impose his own order on history and failed. In Solzhenitsyn's story, General Blagoveschenskii, along with others, attempts to follow the Kutuzov of Tolstoy's writing. Solzhenitsyn depicts him as living in a world of misinformation and illusion. The end is tragedy. In direct contradiction to Tolstoy, Solzhenitsyn concludes that Kutuzovism is a cardinal sin.[12] Character and determination can change events. Leaders influence their own destiny as well as that of others within the broad currents of history. They can and must accept responsibility.

Solzhenitsyn's God

Schmemann emphasizes that for Solzhenitsyn, the roots of defeat are not where Tolstoy or Dostoevsky would have put them. Tolstoy's sense of love, fairness and kindness is not unacknowledged any more than Dostoevsky's fear that the demon of revolution can bring about something even worse. It is the myth of pseudo-messianism and pseudo-mysticism which Solzhenitsyn resists as a deceit. Blame for defeat is not to be put on outsiders any more than it can be excused by recourse to the will of God. Schmemann sums up:

> Reading Solzhenitsyn, one understands with trepidation why it was forbidden ancient Israel to utter the name of God. No, Solzhenitsyn's God is not the God to be used to excuse human irresponsibility, or to obscure truth and justify senselessness; or the God in whose name one hates another while loving and lauding himself. . . . The God of Solzhenitsyn is the living and true God, "ineffable, incomprehensible, invisible and unfathomable." . . . God, Who Is. Thus, in the last analysis, Solzhenitsyn "liberates" even religion from the petty human idolatry which has encrusted it, from its submission to oneself and to one's own, from everything essentially pseudo-religious and pseudo-Christian in it. . . . Purifying religion, Solzhenitsyn sets it again at the center of all.[13]

Schmemann concludes:

> He exposes . . . as false and ruinous, as one about which
> both titans, for all their awesome and permanent truth
> about other and more important things, were *wrong*. The
> false myth, perhaps did not originate with them, but de-
> veloped gradually in the Russian consciousness.[14]

On this view, there is a drastic break between Solzhenitsyn
and his predecessors. Both Tolstoy and Dostoevsky believed that their nation had a peculiar, sanctified destiny.
Governed by a unique spirit, its citizens are endowed with
unmatched—but generally undefined—spiritual perception. In spite of all indebtedness to both Tolstoy and
Dostoevsky, Solzhenitsyn knows that the Tolstoy-Kutuzov
faith in the mysterious and ineffable spirit of Russia has
failed.

Solzhenitsyn's Personal Life

The national experience reflects and has a kind of parallel with Solzhenitsyn's personal life. He states explicitly
that his earlier pattern of thought and feeling underwent
spiritual transformation in imprisonment. Rebirth began
on the day of his arrest. Imprisonment is the most important thing that happened to him in his entire lifetime. Deprived of external freedom, he came to know truth through
suffering. He was uplifted spiritually and came in touch
with reality. Solzhenitsyn speaks of his first cell as his first
love. Only there did he begin to know his own inner life.
The Hebrew-Christian warning against idolatry became
meaningful: only God is absolute. To make any other reality ultimate is self-defeating. From this knowledge, Solzhenitsyn's slavery to Marxism dissolved. Indeed, he was
liberated from all ideology. Solzhenitsyn is emphatic that
Christianity is not an ideology. On the contrary, it is the
destruction of ideology. Accepting the neighbor without
class hatred, it makes possible communication with persons as persons. Authentic growth becomes possible as life

is embraced inclusively. Ideology gives at most a partial
view of reality, indeed a distorted one. Christianity, by
contrast, is for Solzhenitsyn a living spiritual force with
healing power. Through it man can become truly respon-
sive and responsible, in fact, spiritually transformed.

Solzhenitsyn has commented in detail on the religion of
the work camps in *The Gulag Archipelago*.[15] More than
Ivan Denisovich, the majority of prisoners succumbed, becoming victims psychologically, spiritually, often physically.
Christians like Alyosha continue to be present in the camps.
However, such believers do not make up the main body
of prisoners. Solzhenitsyn reports that the dominant religion of the zeks is a demoralized atheism—fatalism which
is without hope for the future. The urge for survival—at
any cost—is dominant. To be sure, there is also a lingering
hope for a kind of redemption, that is, simply for amnesty.
Yet the prisoners know better than to rejoice. Reduced to
less than an animal, most zeks lose all sense of anything
more than day by day existence. The basic rule runs—if
someone gives you something, take it; if he beats you, run.
An attitude of closedness is at the root of the zek's response.
He does not reveal his inmost thoughts. Solzhenitsyn sums
up the matter as follows: zeks belong to an atheistic people
who do not believe the biblical word, "Judge not that ye be
not judged." For the majority, this is laughable. There is no
judgment.

In the end, the walls of Solzhenitsyn's prison cell gave
him understanding. His observations are autobiographical,
taken from his own experience. Reflection for the victim
begins even when he is in transport.[16] A desire for life at any
price wells up within his spirit. Solzhenitsyn emphasizes
that the decisive watershed is at this point. Most zeks never
get beyond this rudimentary urge to continue living whatever the cost. But some souls are deepened. Dostoevsky is a
classical example. Solzhenitsyn explains that imprisonment
can teach one to listen to his inner voices.[17] There are no
meetings or assemblies; no one urges the proletariat to sup-

port the Party line or calls for "voluntary" organization. There is no socialist duty, no elected office to be sought, no criticism of mistakes or interview with local reporters. Family and property have been taken away.

The Gulag Archipelago is not only a report, a record for history. Solzhenitsyn's mood is one of reflection about his data, but also of confession. We cannot say whether he knows Augustine's writings in detail, although he does make passing reference to this Western Church Father. But the important similarities with Augustine's *Confessions* in Solzhenitsyn's writings should not be overlooked. Augustine's introspection is singularly powerful as he tells his sins to God, asking repentance. This kind of reflection is also present in passages of *The Gulag Archipelago*. Like Augustine, Solzhenitsyn makes apparently minor passing events a key to lasting religious insight. Augustine used the incident of his youth—a group of boys wantonly steal and destroy pears—as epitomizing the sheer maliciousness of sin. Solzhenitsyn tells of the evil man who threw tobacco into the eyes of a monkey and blinded it; there is no real explanation apart from the fact of his wickedness. As in the case of Augustine, Solzhenitsyn introspects and examines his own motives intensely. He recalls how he refused to carry the pack of a German prisoner in need. His indifference was a relatively small part of the inhumanity of warfare. The man, tired and emaciated, later met him and smiled. Solzhenitsyn takes this as a gesture of forgiveness. He also remembers that he ordered soldiers to do repair work under shellfire. The wrong remains and must not be forgotten.

Solzhenitsyn and Confession

Solzhenitsyn will confess his own sins to God—the living God who is both righteous judge and redeemer. Like Augustine he recognizes that wickedness is not simply an individual phenomenon. He confesses the sins of his people as well as the nation. Men live together in evil, oppressed by ideologies which pervert whole eras and cultures. Confession is salutary and necessary. Without it there can be no healing. Millions of citizens were accomplices in the crimes of Stalinism. "Only through the repentance of a multitude of people can the air and soil of Russia be cleansed, so that a new, healthy national life can grow up." [18]

For Solzhenitsyn, evil is always personal. It would be impossible without human freedom. In its brute facticity, evil simply is and persists in spite of the Revolution. Solzhenitsyn's experience has been such that he will not affirm progress either in the Western Enlightenment or Marxist sense. Time is not redemptive in and of itself. On the contrary, it can bring even greater wickedness and tragedy. Solzhenitsyn understands with Paul that to know the good is not necessarily to do it. The problem was identified in the Epistle to the Romans and is at the root of the Christian doctrine of sin. Evil is not to be explained from economics but from the spiritual freedom which God has given to men and which they pervert. Solzhenitsyn believes that there is a threshhold over which, having passed, men cannot return. Sin destroys their knowledge, and they are given over to it, as in the case of Stalin. In the past great sinners such as Shakespeare's Iago knew their wickedness. Now, moderns have an ideology which blinds them to sin. Marx's belief that human nature would be reformed when the abuse of religion is restrained is itself a myth, disproved by Stalinism. The so-called natural world is tooth and claw—it is fallen. Human nature is much more morally mixed than he supposed, in short, it needs redemption.

Solzhenitsyn has known the kind of radical evil which cannot be dismissed as just imperfection. But its very degradation made him conscious of a higher source; he has been haunted by the image of perfection. Living personal perfection is at the center of the universe. Where can this vision be seen—in a child, he replies. The child's humanity is an image of eternity. Children do not throw tobacco into the eyes of a monkey—only evil men do. In his letter to Patriarch Pimen, Solzhenitsyn recalls the saving grace of the experience of his own childhood. The child is open to God; it can also recognize evil. There is mystery but also knowledge. Art carries the stamp of authority; its power is spiritual. It can arouse man's ethical concern as well as faith in a higher power. Men have been struck dumb by evil in the twentieth century. Art can bring relief; in it, freedom and perfection are together.

A Sense of Destiny

For Solzhenitsyn, man does not live simply in dependence on science and reason. All experience cannot be controlled simply or manipulated at will. Instead, he has a sense of destiny and providence. Haugh writes:

> Solzhenitsyn's vision of the source of art and value is ultimately rooted in his belief in the Absolute. In an unambigious text from his Nobel Lecture Solzhenitsyn states that the artist has not "created this world, nor does he control it: *there can be no doubts about its foundations*." For Solzhenitsyn the world is a created world. It is a world which might not have existed at all and hence it points beyond itself to its spiritual source. The world, for Solzhenitsyn, is necessarily dependent and participatory, deriving its value and meaning from the uncreated and eternal.[19]

Solzhenitsyn is fully serious in affirming that the soul is illumined by God. Grace and power are given with insight. Solzhenitsyn uses figures of sight and vision, acknowledging the light that lighteth every man that comes into the world. His vision is one of perfection amid imperfection, of the absolute and the relative. Haugh explains that

> The repeated use of certain words—"sight," "gaze," "vision," the "eye," the "heart"—links Solzhenitsyn, perhaps quite unconsciously and unintentionally with that revelatory epistemology so common in the prescholastic Latin West and in the continuous epistemological tradition

of Eastern Christianity. According to this view, man's
inner being is interiorly illumined by the light of the Divine, allowing man to see and judge the temporal from the
perspective of the eternal.[20]

Solzhenitsyn continues to reflect from a vision of
absolute perfection. The Good cannot be reduced to anything less than what it is or destroyed by evil. Justice will
never reduce to injustice. The positive is prior to the negative. When one recognizes this, he is already on the threshhold of the tension between time and eternity. Solzhenitsyn
also has a sense of beatitude, of the possibility of blessed-
ness which transcends this-worldly happiness or success.
Spirit and not matter is primary; it can be corrupted in
evil or redeemed by grace. For Solzhenitsyn, evil is a
corruption. Yet he is committed to the Eastern Orthodox
view of free will. God does not predestine men to evil.
The image of God continues in man in spite of his fallen
condition. God's grace in creation remains and man can
cooperate with it. Haugh argues that the existence of the
Absolute is intuitively obvious for Solzhenitsyn.

> Solzhenitsyn affirms the existence in tri-unity of Truth,
> Goodness, and Beauty precisely because he accepts the
> existence of the "Absolute" or the "perfect." Where there
> is perfection, truth and goodness necessarily co-exist, the
> "radiance" of which is Beauty.[21]

In his Nobel Prize lecture Solzhenitsyn exclaimed:

> So perhaps the old tri-unity of Truth, Goodness, and
> Beauty is not simply the decorous and antiquated formula
> it seemed to us at the time of our self-confident material-
> istic youth. If the tops of these three trees do converge, as
> thinkers used to claim, and if the all too obvious and the
> overly straight sprouts of Truth and Goodness have been
> crushed, cut down, or not permitted to grow, then perhaps
> the whimsical, unpredictable and ever surprising shoots of
> Beauty will force their way through and soar up to *that
> very spot,* thereby fulfilling the task of all three? [22]

The question is not just one of the continuation of life or of accomplishing results at any price. Once in three years, Solzhenitsyn recounts, his group of zeks was shown a film. A sports comedy, entitled "The First Boxing Glove," it carried the moral that the result was important, even if it was not to one's benefit. Solzhenitsyn had time to reflect at length on this theme and concluded as follows: Of course, for socialism, results are important: a powerfully organized party to destroy the opponent, development of iron and steel production, the building of rockets. But only when one no longer fears threats or seeks reward can he know the meaning of freedom. The urge for results at any price destroys the human image. Not the result but the spirit matters, not the "what" but the "how." When one gives up the desire for life at any price, a kind of inner freedom emerges which transcends time and place. In such circumstances, there are no longer hurried questions and oversimplified answers. One is no longer overcome by wickedness; spiritual growth is possible. In sorrow, he learns to care about others. Lacking personal liberty, he finds friendship. Freedom is known to be more than physical relief.

Recovering from an operation in the camp hospital, Solzhenitsyn spent the late night hours with the physician, Boris Nikolajewitsch Kornfeld. Kornfeld was not the attending physician but a fellow victim of the system. Although his face could not be seen clearly, there was a mystical knowledge in his voice. A man of wide culture, he recounted how he had turned from Jewish belief to Christianity. Kornfeld's claim was that no punishment in this earthly life is unearned. When we see deeply into our past, we know this, he urged. The doctor's life soon was to end. Fearing murder by his enemies, he had remained shut up in the ward for two months. The morning after his visit with Solzhenitsyn, he was reported to have died on the operating table. In retrospect, Solzhenitsyn agrees at least in the affirmation that men are afflicted for earlier misdeeds.

Even though innocent of the charges against him, he probes his own conscience, examining his earlier life as he lies in prison. And he looks back with gratitude and new self-knowledge, realizing that he has an understanding of himself and his strivings not otherwise possible.

The whole of Solzhenitsyn's career during more than half a century of Communist rule cannot be understood apart from the fact of the atheistic persecution of religion. The regime claims normalization. However, apart from knowledge of what has gone on, the greatest destruction of Christianity by violence in the entire history of the faith—one cannot appraise conditions. Today, citizens continue to be imprisoned for their religious convictions—some even in insane asylums.[23] How can an author such as Solzhenitsyn be completely "objective" about the matter? Even if one is neutral or an unbeliever, why should he deny freedom to Christians? The answer to that question reveals the idolatry of totalitarianism amid the tragedy of a whole era of history.

In his *Letter to Soviet Leaders*, Solzhenitsyn wrote:

> This ideology that fell to us by inheritance is not only decrepit and hopelessly antiquated now; even during its best decades it was totally mistaken in its predictions and was never a science. . . .
>
> Then religious persecution, which is very important for Marxism, but senseless and self-defeating for pragmatic state leaders—to set useless good-for-nothings to hounding their most conscientious workers, innocent of cheating and theft. For the believer his faith is *supremely* precious, more precious than the food he puts in his stomach.
>
> Have you ever paused to reflect on why it is that you deprive these millions of your finest subjects of their homeland? . . .
>
> This ideology does nothing now but sap our strength and bind us. It clogs up the whole life of society—minds, tongues, radio and press—with lies, lies, lies. For how else can something dead pretend that it is living except by erecting a scaffolding of lies?[24]

Special Treatment for Solzhenitsyn

Solzhenitsyn was exiled almost forty years to the day after Leon Trotsky. Trotsky, the hero of the Russian civil war, the friend of Lenin, and Stalin's strongest rival, was set on a ship in the Black Sea on February 11, 1929. After years of protest and denunciation against Stalin's dictatorship, he was murdered in Mexico. No other person has been treated with as much care and exiled until Solzhenitsyn. Why should Stalin's successors assign a similar fate to a dissident writer? Solzhenitsyn was put on an airplane under security guard and did not know whether he was travelling East or West—to a new prison camp or to exile—until he arrived at his destination. He was discharged at the Frankfurt airport on February 13, 1974. It is reported that on the Moscow subway, every other copy of *Pravda* was open to the brief announcement of Solzhenitsyn's exile. Will he return to Russia—as he still desires to do? In a century which has seen so much revolutionary change, it is not completely unthinkable that this could come to pass in his lifetime.

Summary

The structure of Solzhenitsyn's belief is clear from his writings. He recalls the first impression made upon him by Christian worship as a youth even before he became conscious of anti-religious propaganda. As he grew up, the religious legacy of his family was almost fully overlaid by Marxist atheism. It was the experience of imprisonment which slowly changed the direction of his life. The basic problem of survival—life and death as well as evil—were raised with intensity. Yet even after he had been in confinement for more than a year, Solzhenitsyn reports, he still defended Communism. Its premises continued to be challenged by a wide variety of his fellow prisoners—scientists, politicians, ex-Party members as well as priests. It was not just their words but Solzhenitsyn's own moral sense, his conscience—the inescapable conviction of right and wrong —which caused him to turn increasingly to religion. Today he views the day of his arrest as the beginning of his penance and conversion. He does not seem to have been a Christian at the time of his release. However, by the time of the publication of *One Day in the Life of Ivan Denisovich*, his first novel, he had come to explicit Christian belief.

For Solzhenitsyn, Christianity has been intrinsic to Russian culture for more than a thousand years. His native land and people cannot be saved without it. He is now a practicing member of the Russian Orthodox communion and shares its inclusive "church-type" piety with sacraments and hierarchy. His Christian conviction came only through personal crisis and after long dialogue and reflection. Scepticism preceded faith. Solzhenitsyn came to recognize its value from the warning of an old Marxist who had known Lenin, "Doubt everything, *doubt everything!*" In time, he also concluded that scepticism does not provide a "firm basis underfoot." His older fellow prisoner also warned against idolatry, of making anything less than deity absolute. Father Schmemann has pointed out how the Christian understanding of creation, the fall, and redemption underlies Solzhenitsyn's writing; he has accepted this analysis. His profound grasp of the reality of evil is exemplified in the figure of a helpless monkey blinded by a wicked man who has thrown tobacco into its eyes. Solzhenitsyn has experienced the brute fact of wickedness throughout his own career, but he affirms Providence as well. Richard Haugh calls attention to the way in which Solzhenitsyn's conviction of the presence of the True, the Good, and the Beautiful helps to explain his own mission as a writer. He shares the illuministic tradition of Eastern Christendom. God is authentically present in human creativity. In spite of all wickedness and suffering, the divine is not absent from the world. Solzhenitsyn's moral sense led him back to God, not just as idea, but to the living God of history and personal experience.

What would happen if all the restrictions on freedom of religion were lifted in the Soviet Union? The world has witnessed drastic and sudden changes in the postwar era. What now seems an improbability ought not to be excluded as fully impossible. In short, what would follow if unrestricted worship and discussion of religion were to be allowed and all limits on the training of clergy or the building of churches removed? There is every indication that the churches would be filled as in the war period. New clergy and buildings would be needed. The question of pluralism would emerge if there were no establishment. Would Christianity sectarianize as much as in postwar Japan? The answer is that it probably would not: there is a larger base for unity in Orthodoxy. Problems of ecumenism and clericalism might appear with the growth of tolerance. But the existential questions of the meaning of human life and suffering could be faced freely, no longer defined dogmatically in state propaganda. Is liberty of conscience negotiable? Solzhenitsyn thinks not. The answer depends on how one values man himself. Solzhenitsyn's experience bears witness to the fact that in the case of belief in man and God—faith in one is rooted in the other.

CHAPTER XI

ALEKSANDR SOLZHENITSYN'S
Letter to the Third Council
of the Russian Church Abroad

(Translated from the daily newspaper *Novoe Russkoe Slovo*, September 27, 1974) [1]

Your Eminences, Venerable Fathers, Ladies and Gentlemen:

His Eminence Metropolitan Filaret has asked me to present to you my own views as to how the portion of the Russian Orthodox Church that exists in freedom can render assistance to the oppressed and captive portion in Russia. While acknowledging the fact that I am poorly qualified to speak on ecclesiastical matters before an assembly of clergymen and life-long servants of the Church, I nevertheless feel obligated to accept this invitation. I only ask your forbearance for any errors in terminology or in the substance of the opinions here expressed.

The sad picture of the suppression and destruction of the Orthodox Church on our country's soil has accompanied my entire life from the first impressions of childhood. I recall armed guards marching up to the altar of a church and interrupting the liturgy. I recall an Easter procession being disrupted by people who snatched away candles and Easter cakes. My classmates in school once tore a crucifix from me. Church bells were thrown to the ground, church buildings torn down for bricks. And I remember vividly the pre-war period, when religious services were forbidden practically everywhere in our country. In my hometown, with its population of one half million, there was not a single functioning church. This was thirteen years after the declaration of

Metropolitan Sergius. We must therefore admit that this declaration, far from saving the Church, amounted to an unconditional surrender enabling the authorities to destroy the Church quietly and "without friction." The restoration of the Church three years later was not the result of a concordat between the Church and the authorities, but was merely a response to the disastrous situation threatening the government. The rulers were faced with a powerful wave of religious sentiment throughout the country, they were intimidated by the restoration of churches in the areas occupied by the enemy, and they were forced to seek favorable public opinion in the West. In fact, however, the concessions and promises of 1943 were a deception. The authorities continue to oppress and persecute the Russian Church with the same arrogant, atheistic malice. They tolerate the Church (or so they think) only to the extent that it is necessary for political decoration and as a means of interfering in the affairs of international Orthodoxy.

The Church Is Growing Stronger

However, certain phenomena, especially spiritual, possess their own unpredictable course. The Church, used by Stalin as a pawn in a political game, began to gather strength. As a spiritual body, if not as a formal organization, the Church attained a measure of strength never intended by the authorities, who no longer fully controlled it. Cities are taken by surprise, as the proverb says. By the same sort of surprise our Church was crushed and flattened in the 1920s by forces whose ferocious excesses were committed against an unsuspecting and peaceful people. It is true that the ferocity of the persecution produced a purifying outburst of faith and martyrdom not seen for a long time in the Russian Church or, for that matter, in all of Christendom, but those who confessed their faith were almost completely annihilated. Steadfast worship cost one his freedom, even his life. By the late 1930s it seemed that not only the mass and the tolling of church bells, but even private, whispered prayer, were banished from Russia. But once burnt twice cautious; the Church would not allow itself to be destroyed a second time. We, the people, also grew hardened and resourceful in the atmosphere of Communism, as you can judge from the current social developments in our country. On the other hand, the authorities become from year to year more decrepit, and they grow ever fonder of material wealth. But what in the thirties seemed a doomed spiritual wasteland, today flourishes in many places and spreads in many directions. With recent experiences fresh in my mind, I can attest to the fact that Orthodox churches in the Soviet Union today are like islands, completely set apart from ordinary Soviet life with its Soviet mentality. These churches have been so dispersed across the face of our country that it is sometimes necessary to travel over a hundred miles in order to attend services. Often people are unable to attend church in person; they ask others to say the prayers for the dead and to offer candles. Even the overcrowding in the surviving churches on holy days works against the interests of the oppressors, for in the midst of the current castration of faith in the West, there are probably nowhere else on earth such crowded churches as in the USSR. Faith does not suffer when there is scarcely enough space to bow to the ground or to make the sign of the cross. Standing together shoulder to shoulder we support one another against persecution. And the number of faithful far exceeds the number who are willing and able to attend services. In the Ryazan region, with which I am most familiar, more than seventy per cent of all infants are baptised, despite all the prohibitions and persecution. In the cemeteries crosses are replacing the Soviet markers with their star and photograph. Of course the Church is far from recovered, for it is infiltrated by government informers and it is deprived of all sorts of civil rights. Priests must endure the whims of atheistic petty tyrants. Parishes do not really exist, and the paths to Christian education for our youth have been sealed off, but Russian young people are finding the way to church on their own.

Here I must make a comparison. Sixty or eighty years ago the Russian Orthodox Church, fully supported by a powerful government and with all its power and glory, was shunned and subjected to ridicule by young people and the intelligentsia. There comes to mind a recently deceased pillar of Soviet culture who, having been forced to attend a church service during his youth, placed cigarette butts instead of coins in the church plates, thereby eliciting the admiring laughter of other schoolboys. Today, on the other hand, the intelligentsia and young people in the USSR, many of whom do not share our faith, pay it fitting respect while heaping their ridicule and contempt on the ruling Communist ideology. I remember very well how many fiery adherents were claimed by militant atheism in the 1920s. Those who then went on rampages, blew out candles, and smashed icons with axes have now crumbled into dust, like their Union of the Militant Godless. The more zealous died in that same archipelago as did the faithful clergy. Others repented as their former doctrine lost its momentum, but the Church endured cruelties that seemed unendurable, yet it still stands, albeit far from its natural size. It grows stronger in the fervor of its believers and converts, if not in its formal organization.

The Russian Church Is Not "Fallen"

This is the way I view the contemporary Russian Church in our country, and I should caution those active in the Church abroad against the myopic view that our immense Church is "fallen" and against any attempt to distinguish between this Church and a "true", "clandestine", or "subterranean" Church. In the first fifteen or twenty years of Soviet rule, in the midst of a veritable orgy of oppression, there was some similarity to the church of the catacombs in the secret, underground worship of hounded priests and

persecuted believers. But daily life goes on. The majority
of people are not saints but ordinary mortals, and religion
must attend to their ordinary lives without always demand-
ing heroic feats. If people see a church illuminated by
candles, they will be drawn to it. I am acquainted with
women who in the 1930s harbored priests and arranged
secret religious services in their apartments. Today these
women simply walk to the nearest church. If instead of a
normal church service, there should take place a reading of
prayer books in some deserted place, such as in a cemetery
or on a river bank (I know of such occurrences in the Ryazan area), this would indicate that there are no functioning
churches or available clergymen in the area. It would be a
mistake to infer from such occurrences the existence of
some "secret church organization" as a "nationwide phenomenon." If the authorities were to board up all the
churches tomorrow, underground services would again arise,
but the authorities no longer have the energy to do this.
There is no reason to replace the real Russian Orthodox
people with some imaginary vision of an underground
church. One should not ignore, as some of you have done
in your writings, the existence of the Orthodox community
that has risen independently and grown strong in our country. Today you have a more complex, but at the same time,
more rewarding task than the expression of your solidarity
with a mysterious, sinless, but quite imaginary church of
the catacombs.

The contemporary Church in our homeland is captive,
persecuted, oppressed, but far from fallen! It was resur-
rected by spiritual strength of which, as we can see, God
did not deprive our people. As I have already stated, I cannot ascribe its resurrection and current condition to the
correctness of the program enunciated by Metropolitan
Sergius Stragorodsky and his followers. The body of Christ's
Church was not restored by their pinning to their chests the
medals minted by the Antichrist; nor by luring emigres to
their death in the concentration camps of the homeland;

nor by slanderous propaganda against "bacteriological war-fare conducted by the Americans;" nor by their fainthearted capitulations; nor by their sins. But this was the course followed by those leaders whose historical mission was to act as the spokesmen of divine providence. The sins of sub-missiveness and treachery are borne by the leaders of the Church hierarchy in the form of earthly and heavenly ac-countability, but these sins are not borne by the body of the Church, by the majority of the priesthood, or by the masses who worship in churches. The whole history of Christianity persuades us that these sins can never be transferred to the believers. If the sins of the Church hier-archy were transferred to the Christian people, then there would be no eternal and invincible Church of Christ. In-stead, the Church would be constituted totally by fortuity and the will of individuals.

In order to understand or sympathize with our situation, one must have some knowledge of our recent history. I bow down to the memory of Patriarch Tikhon. What a sense of unfamiliarity, of entering uncharted regions, and of gravity must have attended his progress through those disorderly years, exceeding in violence anything Russia had experi-enced for a thousand years. When, for instance, he raised his hand above the ambo to anathematize the Bolshevik commissars, and when he was racked by doubts while caught in the clutches of Lenin and Trotsky, who were playing their shameless games with the property of the Church: mercy would lead to destruction, but obduracy seemed un-Chris-tian. And also, when, in order to subdue the insolent "reno-vators", he adopted a tone of partial conciliation with the atheist government and when he pondered the advantages and disadvantages of the proffered concessions. On his shoulders rested the weight not only of those unusual years, but also the burden of sins committed in the preceding his-tory of the Russian Church. The sudden death of the Patri-arch (in all probability he was murdered by the CheKa) only lends support to the correctness of his policies. The

rectitude of thousands of priests, monks, bishops, even of
the Patriarch's servant Pyotr, was likewise fatally corrobo-
rated in the prisons of the G.P.U., on the Solovetsky Islands,
in other camps, and in exile. Whoever reveres their steadfastness must weep at the false policy of accommodation
begun by Metropolitan Sergius and continued, even intensified, by his followers. But would they be able to understand
that the inevitable rebirth of the Church had nothing to do
with their endorsement of that policy? On the contrary, they
would have restored the Church with greater success and
glory had they refused all concessions to the Bolsheviks.
We in Russia were the first to learn that one may not make
the slightest spiritual obeisance to a force harmful to the
people. The ultimate result of such a policy is self-destruction. Under such authority we obtain freedom only by
being firm or when such freedom is advantageous to the
authorities. We would never have received anything through
good will. In recent years, given the distribution of strengths
and weaknesses in Russia, the patriarchate in Moscow, with
perhaps the loss of a few positions, could have rid our
Church of many fetters and humiliations by being less sub-
missive. I still feel the same as I did when I wrote my letter
to Patriarch Pimen two years ago. Who should be the first
to call for liberation from lies, if not the fathers of the
Church? However, upon leaving our country I was deprived
of the opportunity to reiterate the stand taken in my letter.
Upon leaving Russia, after having heard only vague rumors
about the divisiveness in the Russian Church abroad, one
is amazed at the depth of the disagreements within Orthodoxy, and also at the gravity of the crisis within the Russian
Church. They have their sorrows there, here we have our
own.

I also found it difficult to understand the leadership of
the Western archbishoprics within the jurisdiction of Moscow. How is it that their compassion for captives leads them
not to strike off their shackles, but to place them on their
own ankles? Their compassion for slaves causes them to

place a yoke on their own necks. Their sympathy for those who must endure lies in captivity leads them to spread these lies in freedom. If these actions are occasioned by devotion to the Mother Church, if all these sacrifices are intended to strengthen unity within the Church, then what we have here is a sorry kind of unity, a perverse illusion that elicits no gratitude from me as a worshipper in the captive branch. If they wish to show solidarity and compassion for us, why do they not speak out clearly against the baseness and deceit of all the groups like the Committee on Church Affairs?

How Can We Justify the Discord Within the Church?

How can we justify the disagreements within the *free* Russian Orthodox churches abroad? I must humbly reiterate my statement made at the beginning of this address: I am by no stretch of the imagination a specialist on ecclesiastical matters. I have never studied canon law. I cannot at the present time go into detail about the history of the Russian churches outside the homeland over the past fifty years. I am, however, familiar with the major points of the discord, and it seems to me that each of the quarrelling factions have considerable canonical basis for their views, and each faction can point to shortcomings in the actions of the other factions (such as the violations of tradition by the Moscow patriarchate). One cannot expect to uncover unquestionable or unconditional canon laws, but without something of the sort the Russian Church could not have survived an epoch of such unforeseeable upheavals. The calculations of architects must take into account ordinary forces of nature, but should the earth itself be cleaved one may not reproach the builders or complain about their calculations. I believe that in such an epoch the canonical foundations must be given less emphasis than the *spirit* of each church and the fidelity of its worship. I should not think that anyone accuses the churches shepherded by Metropolitan Eulogius or by the American Met-

ropolitan of submissiveness to the forces of godlessness or
of cooperation with them, and both offer prayers for the
suffering Russian Church and our persecuted people. Fur-
thermore none of the three quarrelling branches of our
Church can claim to be without error in all its actions. And
who among our countrymen of the last sixty years, either
in the homeland or abroad, has not from time to time enter-
tained illusions, or been in error, or stumbled? No one possesses purity sufficient to call for the expulsion of any
branch from the united Church. I trust that I will not anger
this exalted body by saying this, but it is clear to a new-
comer, to an ignoramus, to a blind person, or to a child,
that the disharmony has hindered the communion between
priests on liturgical matters and even on matters of general
interest. It has led to the shunning of a believer for having
worshiped our God in a different church, even to the refusal
of sacraments to a dying Christian who is somehow not
completely "ours"! This strikes not only at the heart of
Orthodox unity, the common inheritance of Patriarch Tikhon, but at our Christianity itself. Do we alone pray to
Christ? Are all who now worship in the Russian land excommunicated and damned? If they are not condemned, why
are worshippers in the "Parisian" and American churches
condemned?

Coming from the rubble and martyrdom of the captive
Church, one wonders what there is to feel happy about in
the free Church. Which is the more real danger for Russian
Orthodoxy, external oppression in captivity or internal de-
cay through discord? Speaking personally, I never lost hope
in the former situation, but the latter possibility has brought
me to despair. I am comforted only by my impression that
the faithful parishioners here know as little about, and are
as little responsible for, the divergence of opinion in the
hierarchy as are our own inside Russia. It is easy enough
to understand the dedicated stand of the Church in exile
against the tormentors of our people (for which the Soviet
leaders have so persistently striven to neutralize you and

suppress the news), but it is quite impossible to understand why Orthodox groups should consistently be fighting one another. Is the future of Russian Orthodoxy hopeless? If there can be no unity on a small scale within the matrix of common experience, then how much more impossible it is to arrive at a concensus on a large scale in the face of strikingly dissimilar backgrounds.

A detailed study would probably reveal many private, particularistic, personal, psychological, accidental, and petty factors which have deepened and exacerbated the schism in the Church outside Russia. But putting aside every other path to the truth, there arises before us, like an erected cross, a highly perplexing question that we are spiritually obliged to answer without evasion: did this schism arise outside Russia solely as the result of abnormal conditions attributable to emigration? Was the schism not the consequence of the weakened and internally undermined condition that the Russian Church had long suffered? And if the Church was weak, how long had the process gone on?

For many years I have devoted my life to the study of recent Russian history. More precisely, I have sought to learn why the destructive Revolution took place. I have tried to trace the course taken by the Revolution and to determine whether there is a path that would lead Russia from this gangrene to salvation. During the course of this study, I discovered that all sides produced perversions of history and self-serving legends. I would be inconsistent and without hope of ever discovering the truth if, in enumerating these distortions, I were to withhold anything. One of the distortions of history is the depiction of the pre-Revolutionary Russian Church as perfect and needing only to be recreated in its pre-Revolutionary form. The truth requires me to state that the condition of the Russian Church at the beginning of the twentieth century *is one of the principal causes for the inevitability of the Revolutionary events*. The clergy had led a wretched existence for a century. The Church was oppressed by the state and in

collusion with the state. It had lost its authority among
the educated classes and the urban workers and, worst of
all, its authority was tarnished even among the peasantry
(how many proverbs ridicule the priesthood, how few hold
it in respect!). Had the Russian Orthodox Church at the
beginning of the twentieth century been spiritually independent, healthy, and strong, it would have been able to
stop the Civil War. It would have risen above the warring
factions without becoming an appendage to any of them.
This is no fantasy, for in a true Orthodox realm, no such
war of annihilation could have erupted.

The condition of the Russian Orthodox Church at the
time of the Revolution was by no means equal to the gravity
of the spiritual dangers menacing our century and our
people. The Church leaders, having initiated the salutary
reforms and the Church Council, were weighted down by a
complacent governing apparatus and mired in the somno-
lent good humor of their servants. They failed—how visibly
they failed—to prevent the artillery of the Red Guards
from damaging the roof and the cupolas of the very building
in which the Council held its sessions.

In this brief address there is not enough time to speak in
greater detail of the shortcomings within our Church as it
faced the dread year of 1917. Perhaps we could make an
instructive comparison with the shortcomings of the present
patriarchate in Moscow, but those assembled here know
more about this than I, some through personal experience.
But I would call the attention of this assembly to another,
more remote, sin of the Russian Church, a sin of three
hundred years' standing. I stress the word "sin" so as not
to have to use a worse term. The sin of which I speak is one
for which our Church and the entire Orthodox people *have
never repented*. In other words this sin is hanging over our
deliberations here, as it was in 1917. It may, in accordance
with the tenets of our faith, have brought forth God's
retribution in the form of the misfortunes visited upon us.

I have in mind, of course, the Russian inquisition, the

coercion and subjugation of an upright and ancient faith, the persecution and savage treatment of twelve million of our brothers, coreligionists, and compatriots, whose tongues were torn out, who were subjected to pincers, the rack, and death, whose places of worship were destroyed, and who were banished thousands of miles from their homes. They never revolted or took up arms in reply. I cannot bring myself to call these sturdy, faithful, ancient-orthodox Christians by a name like "schismatic." I avoid even calling them Old Believers, for in that case what are we but New Believers, Simply because they did not possess sufficient spiritual agility to accept the hasty and dubious recommendations of those who had visited the Greek patriarchs, because they retained the practice of crossing themselves with two fingers, the means by which our whole church of the seven capitals made the sign of the cross, because of these things we condemned them to punishments just as harsh as those dealt us by atheists under Lenin and Stalin. And yet our hearts have never quivered with repentance! Even today when the faithful gather at Sergiev Posad prayers are read constantly over the remains of Sergius of Radonezh, yet the religious books used by him were said to have been inspired by the Devil and were tossed into bonfires. This unjustifiable persecution, tantamount to the self-destruction of the Russian spirit, Russian integrity, and Russian roots, has continued for 250 years, not the mere sixty of the Soviet persecution. Could the Soviet oppression not have been imposed on us as retribution? In recent centuries other emperors have been inclined to stop persecuting their loyal servants, but the members of the Orthodox hierarchy consulted with one another in whispers and decided that the persecutions would continue. We have had 250 years in which to repent, but we have only found it in our hearts to *forgive the persecuted*, to absolve them as we destroy them. This decision was taken in the year 1905—how the numbers burn in the wall like the warning to Belshazzar! For 250 years we have squandered with careless magnanimity the lives of our Orthodox brethren and those of countless sectarians, and during the Soviet period we have wasted the purest, most zealous and fearless of Russian youth. I believe that the blame for these losses lies not so much with their own actions and beliefs, as with the obduracy, flabbiness, and indifference of the Church.

A Call for Church Unity

The disunity within the Church and our own personal guilt are to some measure responsible for the fate that has befallen Russia. Before us appears a series of steps leading to ultimate unity. By ascending these steps we could truly come together as a United Russian Orthodox Church, worthy at last of God's mercy. Less than a year ago I had the opportunity to observe our most ancient branch at religious services and in conversations at their churches in Moscow, and I can bear witness to their religious devotion and tenacity (against the oppression of the state they are more tenacious than we!), and to their preservation of the Russian character, speech, and spirit in a form found nowhere else on the territory of the Soviet Union. What I saw and heard there convinces me that the unity for which we all pray will not be complete until we are joined in mutual forgiveness with our most ancient branch.

We must climb so many steps before we arrive at brotherhood and love, yet we are stuck on the lowest step in incomprehensible disagreements that have nothing to do with faith, even the subtleties of faith, or ritual, but with *jurisdiction*, a loathesome word never uttered by the lips of Christ nor found in holy writ.

Since the shiny bauble of unlimited material progress has led all of humanity into a depressing spiritual cul-de-sac, represented with only slight nuances of difference in the East as in the West, I can discover only one healthy course for everyone now living, for nations, societies, human organizations, and above all else for churches. We must confess our sins and errors (our own, not those of others), repent, and use self-restraint in our future development. This solution should be applied universally. There is no reason to think that it should not apply to the Russian Orthodox Church, whether free or captive, in exile or in the homeland. The sins of centuries rest on our heads. No tendency or organization within the Church is free of them. All of us together comprise Russia, and we have made it what it is today. You are familiar with my convictions, and of course you will not doubt that I am in complete agreement with the unyielding stand against tyrannical atheism taken by you today. But, for some strange reason, every stand must be developed in order that its basic tenets should not be distorted. The sensitive development of your own views and of the practical measures taken in your individual bishoprics could make your work more effective and could vitally assist the regeneration of the Russian Church.

I may appear to have avoided the question originally put to me, namely: how can the free branch of the Russian Church help the branch in captivity? I will attempt to answer this question as forcefully as I can.

Almost without exception, the fundamental movements determining the future of a country or people take place in metropolitan centers rather than in any sort of diaspora. All who choose exile are paid in the same coin: their influence on their country's fate is diminished. Hence the long sought after liberation of our Church and nation, movements that are making progress at this very minute, will take place in the metropolis, through internal, divinely conceived, and inscrutable processes, which like all complex movements cannot be predicted by even the most farsighted intellects. On the other hand, the *forms* that will manifest themselves immediately after the liberation are within the reach of our prognostications. But here I must caution any arrogant dreamers against expecting the liberated Orthodox community to fall on its knees and beg the hierarchy of the church in exile to lead it. It is not for earthly scales to gauge whether one individual is worthy of another by virtue of suffering, penance, or faith.

How can we here help those in Russia? By setting an example of steadfastness and irreconcilability? Under the circumstances they would find this unconvincing. The only correct path is the one leading to the merger of all branches of the Russian Church. The doctrines that destroyed our country were nurtured by the idea of consistent disunity. Therefore only the unification of her physical and spiritual forces can restore Russia. And, my compatriots, whoever lives abroad yet continues to think of Russia as his homeland, not as a fond memory of the past, but as a real homeland of the future for his descendants, could not better serve Russia than by preserving in Orthodoxy a repository of unity by which all factions of the Russian Church in exile could converge into a united, harmonious, and youthful Church.

I shall take advantage of the invitation to address the Council in order to issue an appeal. All who are activists rather than antiquarians, and who sincerely wish to help, should address themselves to the *future* rather than the past! Then the causes of the unwarranted schism in the Russian Church in exile will fall away and pale into oblivion, and no longer will culprits be sought for the divisions in the past. In addition, the senseless, superficial, "jurisdictional" disputes, which have nothing to do with the practice of our faith, would disappear. And if at the present time structural union is out of the question, a possibility I can appreciate, it is nevertheless possible for the Council by a single gesture, a single manifesto, to cast aside the mutual hostilities between the various churches, and to remove the constraints on liturgical communion between Orthodox priests, so long as they are obviously not serving the cause of godlessness. I ask you to imagine the sad picture that will greet the ordinary Orthodox Russian in our home-land, when he sees how Orthodoxy is unpardonably split when living without oppression in freedom.

The decisions of this Council cannot determine the future course and the liberation of the Russian Church in the metropolis, but these decisions preordain the form and de-gree of your future influence within the liberated Church.

But is the desired liberation of the Church from the dic-tatorship of the godless really our first and foremost task? The current crisis of the Church, a crisis that is centuries old, is considerably deeper and weighs more heavily upon us than do more transitory problems. Does it take more than sagacious wisdom or moral strength to seek repara-tions for sins, injustices, and errors which are of ancient origin and scarcely remembered today? But each of these transgressions have lain across the face of Russian Ortho-doxy like disfiguring scars. How can we create a Church that will not persecute its own children? How can we make a Church that would not be an instrument of the state, would not be spiritually subordinate to the power of the state, and would not be connected with political parties; a Church in which would flourish the best of our as yet un-implemented reforms, aimed at restoring the purity and freshness of primitive Christianity; a Church that would not merely exist for its own sake, but would assist all of Russia in finding its own, native, distinctive path away from the suffocation and darkness of today's world?

We as the Church must take on a form that is not merely a replica of the pre-Revolutionary Church. We must attain a form that is of such stature and that is so suffused with an unfading sense of searching, that even the Western world, now languishing in an unquenchable spiritual long-ing, will be drawn to us. The incomparable bitterness of the Russian experience indeed holds out such a hope for us.

In conclusion I repeat: I do not presume to decide ec-clesiastical questions. But each layman must speak the

truth as he sees it, in the hope that the wisdom and conscience of the Council will be provided with any information
it might need.

I ask the blessing of the prelates and pastors, and the
prayers of all.

ALEKSANDR SOLZHENITSYN
August, 1974

Notes

Chapter 1

1. Harry Schwartz, "Solzhenitsyn Without Stereotype", *Saturday Review of Literature*, 1:30, April 20, 1974.
2. Milovan Djilas, "Aleksandr the Great," *Book World*, The Washington Post, January 23, 1974, 1.
3. G. F. Kennan, Review of *The Gulag Archipelago, New Republic*, 170:21, June 22, 1974.
4. Aleksandr I. Solzhenitsyn, *The First Circle*, translated by Thomas P. Whitney, Bantam, New York, (1968), 1972, 234–235.
5. *Ibid.*, 450.
6. *Ibid.*, 618.
7. *Ibid.*, 24.
8. Abraham Rothberg, Aleksandr Solzhenitsyn, *The Major Novels*, Cornell University Press, Ithaca, 1971, 9.
9. David Burg and George Feifer, *Solzhenitsyn*, Abacus, London, 1973, 231.
10. Alexander Solzhenitsyn, *Stories and Prose Poems*, translated by Michael Glenny, Bantam, New York, 1973. "Lake Segden," 198.
11. Dan Jacobson, "The Example of Solzhenitsyn," *Commentary*, May, 1969, 82. Cited by Rothberg, *op. cit.*, 17.
12. Alexander Solzhenitsyn, "The Love-Girl and the Innocent," translated by Nicholas Bethell and David Burg, Bantam, New York, 1971, ix.
13. *Aleksandr Solzhenitsyn: Critical Essays and Documentary Materials*, edited by John B. Dunlop, Richard Haugh, and Alexis Klimoff, Nordland, Belmont, Massachusetts, 1973, 497.
14. David M. Halperin, "The Role of the Lie in *The First Circle*," Dunlop, *op. cit.*, 260.

Chapter 2

1. Terrance Des Pres, "The Heroism of Survival," Dunlop, *op. cit.*, 53.
2. Burg and Feifer, *op. cit.*, 261.
3. Luellen Gold Lucid, "The Writer as Public Figure: Mailer, Sartre, Solzhenitsyn: An Essay in the Sociology of Literature," Unpublished dissertation, Yale University, 1973.

4. Alexander Solzhenitsyn, *One Day in the Life of Ivan Denisovich*, translated by Ralph Parker. English translation © copyright 1963 by E. P. Dutton & Co., Inc. and Victor Gollancz, Ltd. Reprinted by permission of the publishers, E. P. Dutton & Co., Inc.
5. Leopold Labedz, *Solzhenitsyn: A Documentary Record*, Harper, New York, 1971, 121.
6. Georg Lukas, *Solzhenitsyn*, tr. William David Graf, MIT Press, Cambridge, Massachusetts, 1971, 13–14.
7. V. Lakshin, *Novy Mir*, January, 1964. Cited by Christopher Moody, *Solzhenitsyn*, Oliver and Boyd, Edinburgh, 1973, 33.
8. Rothberg, *op. cit.*, 34.
9. *One Day*, 154–157.
10. *Ibid.*, 87.
11. *Ibid.*, 84.
12. *Ibid.*, 155–156.
13. Michael Nicholson, "Solzhenitsyn and *Samizdat*," Dunlop, *op. cit.*, 75.
14. *Ibid.*, 82.
15. Dunlop, *op. cit.*, 490.

Chapter 3

1. In an interview published in New Haven *Register*, April 4, 1972. Cited by Lucid, *op. cit.*, 190.
2. Robert Conquest, ed., *The Pasternak Affair, A Documentary Report*, Lippincott, Philadelphia, 1962, 108.
3. Priscilla Johnson and Leopold Labedz, ed., *Khrushchev and the Arts, The Politics of Soviet Culture*, 1962–1964, MIT Press, Cambridge, 1965, 152. Originally in *Pravda*, March 10, 1963.
4. Cited in Burg and Feifer, 358.
5. At the meeting of the Writers' Union reported by Hans Björkegren, *Aleksandr Solzhenitsyn*, The Third Press, New York, 1972. 111.
6. Lucid, *op. cit.*, 306.
7. Johnson and Labedz, *Khrushchev and the Arts*, 272. Originally in *Oklyabr*, No. 10, October, 1963.
8. Burg and Feifer, 290.
9. *Ibid.*
10. Michael Nicholson, "Solzhenitsyn and *Samizdat*," Duncan, *op. cit.*, 69.
11. See *The First Circle*, 324.
12. Burg and Feifer, 287–289.
13. *Ibid.*
14. Björkegren, *op. cit.*, 137–138.
15. *Ibid.*, 165.
16. Burg and Feifer, 409.
17. Labedz, *Solzhenitsyn*, 207–208.

Chapter 4

1. Paul Neuburg, *The Hero's Children, The Post-War Generation in Eastern Europe*, Morrow, New York, 1973, 309.
2. From *The Marxism of Jean-Paul Sartre* by Wilfrid Desan, p. 39. Copyright © 1965 by Wilfrid Desan. Reprinted by permission of Doubleday & Company, Inc.
3. *Ibid.*, 33.
4. *Ibid.*, 32.
5. Neuburg, *op. cit.*, 360.
6. Robert C. Turner, *Philosophy and Myth in Karl Marx*, Cambridge University Press, New York, 1972, 242.
7. Neuburg, *op. cit.*, 309.
8. See *The First Circle*, 58.
9. *Ibid.*, 340.
10. Nikita Struve, "The Debate About *August 1914*," Dunlop, *op. cit.*, 397.
11. *First Circle*, 21–22, 39, 78.
12. *Ibid.*, 50, 481.
13. *Ibid.*, 134.
14. Rothberg, *op. cit.*, 76.
15. *First Circle*, 673–675.
16. *Ibid.*, 397–398.
17. *Ibid.*, 95–96, 636.
18. Des Pres, *op. cit.*, 62.

Chapter 5

1. Introduction to the English translation of Andrei D. Sakharov's *Progress, Coexistence, and Intellectual Freedom*, W. W. Norton & Company, Inc., New York, 1968, 12.
2. Alexander Solzhenitsyn, *Letter to Soviet Leaders*, translated by Hilary Sternberg, Fontana, London, 1974, 46.
3. Quoted from Solzhenitsyn's essay, "On the Return of Breathing and Consciousness," in *From Under the Ruins, Time*, Vol. 104, No. 22, November 25, 1974, 57.
4. Solzhenitsyn, "On the Debasement of the Russian Intelligentsia," *Time*, November 25, 1974, 52.
5. Gleb Struve, "Behind the Front Lines: On Some Neglected Chapters in *August 1914*," Dunlop, *op. cit.*, 443.
6. Chapters from the *Vekhi* have been translated by Marshall Shatz and Judith Zimmerman, and published in the *Canadian Slavic Studies*, from summer 1968 to fall 1972, II, 2 — V, 3.
7. Sergei Bulgakov, "Heroism and Asceticism, Reflections on the Religious Nature of the Russian Intelligentsia," *Canadian Slavic Studies*, III–3 (291–310) 293, III–4 (447–463).

8. Peter Struve, "The Intelligentsia and Revolution," IV–2 (183–198), 193.
9. B. Kistiakovaskii, "In Defense of Law (The Intelligentsia and Legal Consciousness," IV–1 (36–59), 52. Mikhail Gershenzon, "Creative Self-Consciousness," III–1 (1–21), 7.
10. Bulgakov, *op. cit.*, 297.
11. Lenin, *Collected Works*, XVI, 127–128.
12. Semen Frank, "The Ethic of Nihilism: A Characterization of the Russian Intelligentsia's Moral Outlook," V–3 (327–354), 340.
13. Alexander Solzhenitsyn, *The Gulag Archipelago*, tr. Thomas P. Whitney, Collins/Fontana, Glasgow, 1974, 168.
14. Nicolas Berdiaev, "Philosophical Verity and Intelligentsia Truth," II–2, 157–174.
15. Lenin, *op. cit.*, 123–125.
16. H. Montgomery Hyde, *Stalin, The History of a Dictator*, Popular Library, New York, 1971, 225–226.

Chapter 6

1. Rothberg, *op. cit.*, 134.
2. *Cancer Ward*, 74, 78, 137, 209, 255.
3. *Ibid.*, 135.
4. *Ibid.*, 94.
5. *Ibid.*, 437–439.
6. Labedz, *op. cit.*, 120–121.
7. Thompson Bradley, "Aleksandr Solzhenitsyn's *Cancer Ward:*
8. *Ibid.*, 301.
9. Alexander Schmemann, "On Solzhenitsyn," Dunlop, *op. cit.*, 39, 44.
10. *Ibid.*, 41–42.
11. *Ibid.*, 42.

Chapter 7

1. Labedz, *op. cit.*, 194–195.
2. *The First Circle*, 146.
3. Hyde, *op. cit.*, 64.
4. William C. Fletcher, Nikolai, *Portrait of a Dilemma*, Macmillan, New York, 1968.
5. Dunlop, *op. cit.*, 472–477.

Chapter 8

1. Dimitry Konstantinow, *Die Kirche in der Sowjetunion nach dem Kriege, Entfaltung und Rückschläge*, Pustet, Munich, 1973, 16–17.
2. *The Gulag Archipelago*, I–II, 37.

3. Konstantinow, *op. cit.*, 17.
4. *Ibid.*, 43 *et seq.*
5. *Ibid.*, 234.
6. *Ibid.*, 285.
7. *Ibid.*, 353 *et seq.*
8. *The Gulag Archipelago*, I–II, 170–171.
9. *Novoye Russkoyo Slovo* (Russian Daily, New York, Friday, September 27, 1974, 2.
10. *Ibid.*
11. *Ibid.*
12. *Ibid.*
13. *Ibid.*
14. Dunlop, *op. cit.*, 472–744.

Chapter 9

1. V. S. Pritchett, "Reason Devouring its Children," *New Statesman,* June 28, 1974, 925.
2. Robert Conquest, "Evolution of an Exile," *Saturday Review of Literature,* April 20, 1974, 22.
3. Conquest, *op. cit.*, 23.
4. Pritchett, *op. cit.*, 925.
5. *The Gulag Archipelago*, I–II, 489.
6. Hyde, *op. cit.*, 349.
7. *The Gulag Archipelago*, I–II, 130.
8. *Ibid.*, 161–162.
9. *Der Archipel Gulag*, translated into German by Anna Peturnig Scherz, Bern, 1974, III–IV, 26 *et seq.*
10. *Ibid.*, 67 *et seq.*
11. *Letter to Soviet Leaders*, 44–45.
12. *The Gulag Archipelago*, I–II, 174.

Chapter 10

1. Czeslaw Milosz, *The Captive Mind*, translated by Jane Ziclonko, Random House, New York, 1953.
2. Nobel Prize Lecture, Dunlop, *op. cit.*, 491.
3. *Ibid.*, 491–492.
4. *Der Archipel Gulag*, 1974, 593.
5. Czeslaw Milosz, "Questions," Dunlop, *op. cit.*, 454.
6. Wolfgang Leonard, *Three Faces of Marxism,* tr. Ewald Osers, Holt, Rinehart and Winston, New York, 1974, 126–127.
7. Hyde, *op. cit.*, 611.
8. *Ibid.*, 609.
9. *Ibid.*, 95.
10. *Ibid.*, 29.

11. Alexander Schmemann, "A Lucid Love," Dunlop, *op. cit.*, 386.
12. See Alexander Schmemann, "A Lucid Love," 386.
13. *Ibid.*, 391.
14. *Ibid.*, 385.
15. AG, 501–505.
16. AG, 581.
17. AG, 584.
18. Quoted in *Time*, Vol. 104, No. 22, November 25, 1974, 52.
19. Richard Haugh, "The Philosophical Foundations of Solzhenit-syn's Vision of Art," Dunlop, *op. cit.*, 175.
20. *Ibid.*, 177.
21. *Ibid.*, 178.
22. Nobel Prize Lecture, Dunlop, 482.
23. Michael Bourdeaux, *Faith on Trial in Russia*, Harper, New York, 1971.
24. *Letter to Soviet Leaders*, 42–46.

Chapter 11

1. This translation of Solzhenitsyn's open letter to the Russian Emigre Church is included as the final chapter of this book so that you may judge for yourself from his own words the nature of his religion.

   Brief quotations from this letter in Chapter 8 may differ slightly from the wording in this chapter since a different translator made the two translations.

   "Aleksandr" is the commonly used translation of the Russian; elsewhere in this book "Alexander" is used.

   In addition to the publication in Russian in *Novoye Russkoyo Slovo*, this letter has also been translated into French and published in France.